First Star
The Blue-Pillowed Sky
A Shiny Golden Path
Rainbow Bridge
Slide Down the Sky
From Sea to Shining Sea
Time for Dreams
Across the World
Over the Moon
Sound of the Sea
Promises to Keep

O beautiful for spacious skies,
   For amber waves of grain,
For purple mountain majesties
   Above the fruited plain!
      America! America!
   God shed His grace on thee,
And crown thy good with brotherhood
   From sea to shining sea!

—Katharine Lee Bates

From Sea to Shining Sea

An anthology
compiled and edited by

Zena Sutherland and **Marilyn F. Cunningham**

Program Authors

Carl Bereiter
Marlene Scardamalia
Ann Brown
Valerie Anderson
Joseph Campione
Walter Kintsch

Open Court
La Salle, Illinois

President and Publisher
M. Blouke Carus

Education Director
Carl Bereiter

Project Coordination
Marsha Roit

Project Planning and Implementation
Thomas G. Anderson,
Commonwealth Strategies, Inc.

Senior Editor
Marilyn Cunningham

Permissions
Diane Sikora

Art Direction
Todd Sanders

Cover Design
James Buddenbaum

ISBN 0-8126-2215-4

Acknowledgments

Grateful acknowledgment is given to the following publishers and copyright owners for permission granted to reprint selections from their publications. All possible care has been taken to trace ownership and secure permission for each selection included.

Marie F. Brown, for "Brer Possum and Brer Snake," from *The Days When the Animals Talked* by William J. Faulkner; text copyright © 1977 by William J. Faulkner.

Carolrhoda Books, Inc., 241 First Avenue North, Minneapolis, Minnesota 55401: for excerpts from *Deborah Sampson Goes to War* by Bryna Stevens, text copyright © 1984 by Bryna Stevens; and for excerpts from *Keep the Lights Burning, Abbie* by Peter and Connie Roop, copyright © 1985 by Carolrhoda Books, Inc.

Childrens Press: for excerpts from *Martin and Abraham Lincoln* by Catherine Cate Coblentz, copyright 1947 Childrens Press; and for excerpts titled "Westward Ho!" from *The True Book of Pioneers* by Mabel Harmer, copyright 1957 Childrens Press.

Coward, McCann & Geoghegan, for an adaptation of *Lysbet and the Fire Kittens* by Marietta Moskin, text copyright © 1974 by Marietta Moskin.

Dodd, Mead & Company, Inc., for "Journey for Sacajawea," from *The Indians and the Strangers* by Johanna Johnston; copyright © 1972 by Johanna Johnston.

Doubleday & Company, Inc., and William Heinemann Limited, for "City Rain" and "I'd Like to Be a Lighthouse" by Rachel Field, from *Taxis and Toadstools*; copyright 1926 by Doubleday & Company, Inc.

E. P. Dutton, a division of NAL Penguin Inc.: for the poem on page ii ("America the Beautiful"), from *Poems* by Katharine Lee Bates, published in 1926 in the United States by E. P. Dutton, all rights reserved; and for an adaptation of *Watch the Stars Come Out* by Riki Levinson, illustrated by Diane Goode, text copyright © 1985 by Riki Friedberg Levinson, illustrations copyright © 1985 by Diane Goode.

Four Winds Press, an imprint of Macmillan Publishing Company, for "The Apollo Program," adapted from *The Moon* by Seymour Simon; copyright © 1984 by Seymour Simon.

Greenwillow Books, a division of William Morrow & Company, for "Today Is Very Boring," from *The New Kid on the Block* by Jack Prelutsky; text copyright © 1984 by Jack Prelutsky.

Harcourt Brace Jovanovich, Inc., for "Buffalo Dusk," from *Smoke and Steel* by Carl Sandburg; copyright 1920 by Harcourt Brace Jovanovich, Inc., renewed 1948 by Carl Sandburg.

Harcourt Brace Jovanovich, Inc., and The Bodley Head, for an excerpt from *Rufus M.* by Eleanor Estes, copyright 1943, 1971 by Eleanor Estes.

Illustration

Victor Ambrus (54, 55, 56-57, 59), George Armstrong (27, 28), David Beck (cover), Joseph Cellini (91, 118, 120, 122, 168, 180), David Cunningham (160), Susan David (40, 42, 44, 45), Bert Dodson (14, 15, 35, 37, 104-105, 106, 108), Tom Dunnington (79, 80-81, 82, 84), Larry Frederick (16, 17, 18-19), Stephen Gammell (92), Marika Hahn (178), Lydia Halverson (21, 22-23, 124, 125, 126, 128, 131, 132), Dennis Hockerman (30-31, 32, 34), Ann Iosa (152, 154, 156), Jan Naimo Jones (148-149, 151, 179), Joanna Koperska (6, 20, 36, 68), Monica Loomis (137, 139, 140), Giulio Maestro (183, 184), Diana Magnuson (172-173, 176), Stephen Marchisi (93, 96, 97, 98), Bob Masheris (86-87, 88-89, 90, 186, 187), Victor Mays (7, 25), Charles McBarron (9, 10, 69, 71), Yoshi Miyake (24, 46, 47, 48-49, 51, 167), Rodney Pate (99, 101, 102, 103), James Watling (11, 12-13, 72-73, 74-75, 76, 77, 78).

Photography

The Art Institute of Chicago (134, 136), Camera 5, Ken Regain (181), The Gartman Agency (4), Thomas Gilcrease Institute, Tulsa, Oklahoma (53), The Huntington, San Marino, California (133), The Image Bank (5), NASA (2, 163, 165, 166), National Gallery of Art, Washington, D. C. (135), New Mexico Museum, Susan Peterson (159), Wide World Photos, Inc. (169, 171).

Contents

Unit One   Our Country Long Ago

Unit Two   Stories and People

Unit Three   Our Country Grows

Unit Four   Stories and People

Unit Five   Our Country Today

Unit One
Our Country Long Ago

Our Country

How does the United States look to an astronaut high above the earth? What would you see of our country if you were flying around the earth so high in the sky?

If you were an astronaut, you would see the large oceans around the United States. You would also see that almost all of our country is part of a big piece of land that is called North America. You would see Canada to the north of our country and Mexico to the south.

Look at the picture on page 2. This is how our country would look to you from high above the earth. Compare the picture with the map on pages 4–5. Do you see how our country is divided into states? Find the state in which you live.

Did you know that the United States was not always so big as it is today? When our country began, it had only thirteen states. Today it has fifty.

This book will tell you how the United States grew to become the country it is today. It will tell you about our early explorers, our brave pioneers, and our great men and women. You will learn about the Indians, who lived here for thousands of years before the first settlers came. You will also learn about some of the important events in our country's history.

As you read this book, you will understand better why our country is a great country. What you learn should make you very glad that you live in the United States.

This Land Is Your Land

WOODY GUTHRIE

This land is your land—
This land is my land—
From California
To the New York island,
From the redwood forest
To the Gulf Stream waters.
        This land was made for you and me.

As I was walking
That ribbon of highway,
I saw above me
That endless skyway;
I saw below me
That golden valley.
        This land was made for you and me.

I've roamed and rambled,
And I followed my footsteps
To the sparkling sands
Of her diamond deserts;
And all around me
A voice was sounding.
This land was made for you and me.

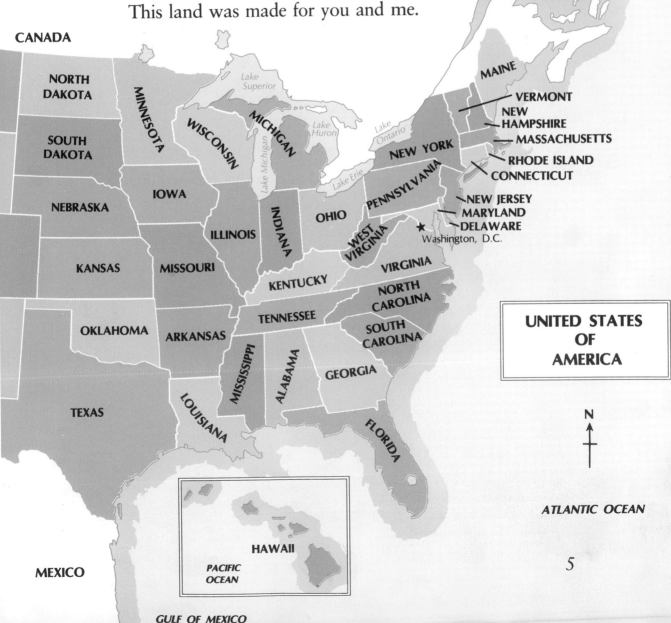

CANADA

NORTH DAKOTA

SOUTH DAKOTA

NEBRASKA

KANSAS

OKLAHOMA

TEXAS

MINNESOTA

IOWA

MISSOURI

ARKANSAS

LOUISIANA

WISCONSIN

MICHIGAN

Lake Superior

Lake Michigan

Lake Huron

ILLINOIS

INDIANA

OHIO

KENTUCKY

TENNESSEE

MISSISSIPPI

ALABAMA

Lake Erie

Lake Ontario

NEW YORK

PENNSYLVANIA

WEST VIRGINIA

VIRGINIA

NORTH CAROLINA

SOUTH CAROLINA

GEORGIA

FLORIDA

MAINE

VERMONT

NEW HAMPSHIRE

MASSACHUSETTS

RHODE ISLAND

CONNECTICUT

NEW JERSEY

MARYLAND

DELAWARE

★ Washington, D.C.

UNITED STATES
OF
AMERICA

N

ATLANTIC OCEAN

HAWAII

PACIFIC OCEAN

MEXICO

GULF OF MEXICO

5

The First Americans

The first people to live in America were the Indians. They were here for thousands of years before white people came.

Look at the map below. You can see that Asia almost touches North America. Most scientists think the Indians came from Asia to North America more than twenty thousand years ago. At that time there was dry land between Asia and North America. The Indians may have followed the animals they hunted across this land bridge.

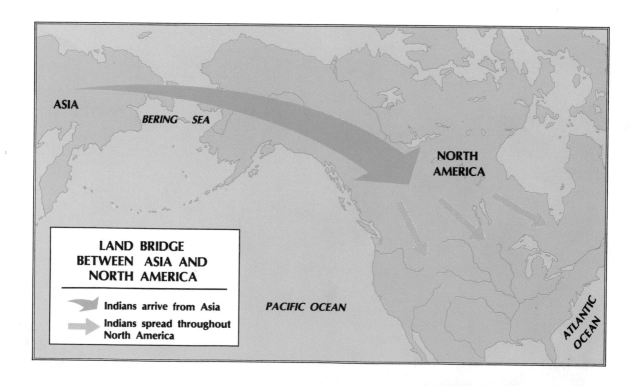

ASIA

BERING SEA

NORTH AMERICA

LAND BRIDGE BETWEEN ASIA AND NORTH AMERICA

➤ Indians arrive from Asia

➤ Indians spread throughout North America

PACIFIC OCEAN

ATLANTIC OCEAN

By the time white people came, different groups of Indians lived in almost every part of North and South America. Each group, or tribe, had its own language and its own way of living. Each had its own artists and workers who used natural materials to make beautiful things.

Some of the Indians were hunters, who wandered the land with their bows and arrows. They made camp wherever the hunting was best. Some were fishermen, who worked from reed boats or bark canoes and lived in settled villages. Others were farmers, who also lived in villages.

These people did not call themselves Indians. That name was given to them by Christopher Columbus. Every tribe had its own special name. The people were very proud of themselves and of their tribes.

The next stories are about some of the North American Indians who lived in what is now the United States.

Indians of the East

The Indians who lived in the eastern part of the United States were hunters and farmers. They tracked animals silently in the thick forests, fished in the swift streams, and grew many crops. People in the East had plenty to eat.

The Indian men did the hunting and fishing, and the women did the farming. They grew corn, tobacco, beans, and squash. They pounded the kernels of corn into meal and boiled it in water to make cornmeal mush.

In the northeast, the Indians made maple sugar from the sap of maple trees. They used this sugar to make their cornmeal sweet. The people who lived near the Great Lakes ate the wild rice that grew in great, swampy fields. And Indians everywhere knew how to make a good meal out of nuts and berries and other wild plants.

Some Indians in the East lived in wigwams, which were small, round houses covered with sheets of bark. One family lived in each wigwam.

Other Indians lived in longhouses, which were long buildings made of logs and bark. Several families lived together in one longhouse.

The Eastern Indians wore clothing made of deerskin or of cloth made from plant fibers. Sometimes they sewed feathers onto netting to make light, warm robes. They made wooden bowls and spoons. Most of them also knew how to make pottery out of clay and how to weave baskets out of many kinds of plants. They used these pots and baskets for gathering and storing food and water.

The roads of that time were the many lakes and rivers in the eastern part of the United States. The Indians traveled along these waterways in canoes made of elm or birch bark.

The canoes traveled quickly over the water and could be easily carried over land to the next river or lake.

In the valleys of the Mississippi and Ohio rivers lived the Indians known as the Mound Builders. They were given that name because of the mounds they built to bury their dead people in. Some of the mounds were eighty feet high.

The Mound Builders lived in log huts. Their towns were surrounded by walls made of stakes. They grew corn, squash, and pumpkins. They spun fibers of nettles, grass, fur, and hair, and then wove cloth from these fibers. These Indians also made beautiful bracelets, breastplates, and helmets out of copper, mica, beaten silver, and pearls. They traded in distant places and formed a great nation stretching over hundreds of miles.

All of the Indians of the East knew how to use the good things that nature gave them.

Indians of the West

Many tribes of Indians lived in the western part of the United States. Some lived along the Pacific Ocean from Alaska to northern California. Fish and game were plentiful on this coast. The Indians speared salmon and other fish in the rivers of the area. They also knew how to hunt seals, sea otters, and even the mighty whale. Thick forests near the ocean supplied them with game, such as deer and elk, and with plenty of plants and berries.

The women of the coastal tribes wove lovely blankets and robes, while the men made beautiful copper shields and wooden masks. The men also made great seagoing canoes from the huge cedar and redwood trees that grew along the coast.

The Indians used their canoes for hunting whales. This kind of hunting was very dangerous because the canoes were much smaller than the whales. When a canoe got close to a whale, the hunters threw their harpoons. Each harpoon had a rope tied to one end. The other end of the rope was tied to the boat. A wounded whale often pulled the canoe far out into the ocean before it died.

Because the Indians of the northwest coast did not have to travel around hunting for food, they built strong houses called *lodges*. Lodges were made of big cedar trees cut down with stone hatchets. They were big enough for many families to live in.

Outside their lodges, the Indians put up totem poles. Totem poles were very tall and had faces and animals carved on them, one on top of another. Each totem pole told the story of a family or clan.

The Indians who lived farther south in California lived in small villages. They ate wild plants, seeds, and nuts. They knew how to pound acorns into flour, which they used to make bread or mush. These Indians also hunted game and fished in the rivers.

Some Indians lived in the high plain between the mountains near the ocean and the Rocky Mountains to the east. This area was too dry to grow crops, and there were not many animals. The Indians learned to survive by eating things like snakes, grasshoppers, and grubs.

Both the California Indians and those of the high plain made beautiful woven baskets. They used feathers and beads to decorate these baskets in wonderful patterns.

Indian Children Long Ago

NANCY BYRD TURNER

Where we play in field and hill,
Running high and low,
Other children used to play,
Long and long ago.

Little Indians straight and slim,
Boys with belt and feather,
Little girls with colored beads,
Playing all together.

Laughing, calling through our yard
(When 'twas field of maize),
Swift and light they used to run,
Back in other days;

Through our garden (once a wood)
In and out again,
Past the house they ran, and back—
'Twas a wigwam then.

Sometimes when the air is clear,
On a quiet day,
We can almost hear them still,
Shouting at their play!

And Then Came Columbus

One sunny day in Italy over five hundred years ago, a boy named Christopher Columbus was sitting on the seashore, looking out over the water.

"I'm going to be a sailor when I grow up," he said to himself. "I want to sail the seas to faraway lands."

Columbus loved the ocean, and when he grew up he did become a great sailor. The place he wanted most to sail to was the Indies, which at that time included Japan, China, and India. These rich countries had many goods to trade.

Christopher Columbus was not only a great sailor. He was a great thinker. His thoughts about going to the Indies must have been something like this: "Everybody else sails to the Indies by traveling east, but that takes too long and costs too much. I think that, in this round world of ours, I can get to the Indies more quickly by sailing west!"

But Columbus was a very poor man. He had no ships and no money. He needed someone else to pay for his trip. Whenever he explained his plan for sailing west, however, people just laughed at him and thought he was strange.

It wasn't that people thought the world was flat or that Columbus would sail off the edge of it. Most educated people at that time knew that the world was round. They even agreed that it just might be possible to reach the Indies by sailing west. But nobody knew how far you'd have to sail to get there. In those days no one knew exactly how big our earth was or how far the oceans went—and those are things you ought to know before you set sail.

But Columbus kept trying to find someone to give him ships and money. Finally, after several years, Queen Isabella of Spain gave him three ships and wished him good luck. Columbus still needed a crew of sailors, though.

Sailors did not want to go on the voyage. They had heard stories about monsters and sea serpents attacking ships in the western sea and killing the sailors. They weren't sure they wanted to head out into an unknown ocean, sailing who knows how far to find the Indies. If they had to sail too long, the ships would run out of food and fresh water long before land was sighted.

Finally Columbus was able to gather a crew of eighty-eight men. His ships were ready, and in 1492 Columbus and his sailors set out across the Atlantic Ocean in the *Santa María,* the *Pinta,* and the *Niña.*

It was a long, long voyage. The ships sailed for many weeks, and the farther they went, the more frightened the sailors became.

At last the sailors said to Columbus, "We have been on the ocean for more than sixty days, and there is still no sight of land. We will go no farther!"

But Columbus answered, "Wait just three more days. If we have not found land by then, we will go home."

The very next day the sailors saw a bird, and they knew that land must be near. The following morning, October 12, 1492, they heard the cry "Land ho!" There ahead of them lay a beautiful island. The sailors cheered and the ships' cannons boomed. When they reached shore, many sailors kissed the ground because they were so glad to be on land again. They asked Columbus to forgive them for wanting to give up the voyage and return home. Then they all set out to explore this marvelous new land.

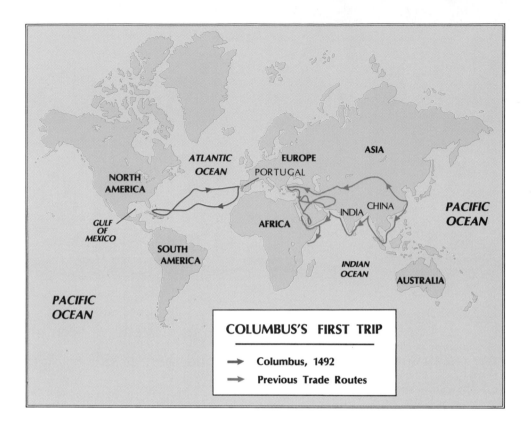

COLUMBUS'S FIRST TRIP

→ Columbus, 1492
→ Previous Trade Routes

Later, Columbus wrote in his journal: "The lands are all most beautiful and full of trees so high they seem to reach to the sky. The nightingale was singing and, too, other birds of a thousand sorts. The people of this island, and of all the others that I have found and seen, are kind and generous with what they have."

Columbus named these people "Indians," thinking that he had landed in the Indies. Little did he dream that he had instead discovered a whole new continent!

The Pilgrims

In the middle of the Atlantic Ocean a little ship was being tossed about in a fierce storm. The lightning cracked, the thunder roared, and huge waves washed over the decks.

"It's a terrible night," said Captain Jones. "I only hope we live through it."

"We'll live through it," replied William Brewster firmly. "Nothing will keep us from reaching America. It is God's will."

The year was 1620, and the name of the little ship was the *Mayflower*. The people on board called themselves Pilgrims, because they had wandered so long looking for a place where they could worship as they pleased.

The Pilgrims had left their native England because the king wouldn't let them practice their religion. Then they had lived in Holland. Finally they were on their way to the new country of America.

For many weeks the *Mayflower* tossed about on the ocean. At last the Pilgrims reached the rocky shore of what is now Massachusetts.

It was the middle of winter, so the Pilgrims—ninety-nine men, women, and children—immediately set out to build themselves a shelter. At first they built one log house big enough to hold everyone, but later they built a house for each family.

The Pilgrims' first winter was a hard one. The weather was cold and bitter, and sometimes they did not have enough to eat. By spring nearly half of them had become sick and died.

The only people the Pilgrims met in this new land were Indians. At first the Pilgrims were afraid of these Indians, but they proved to be helpful and friendly. Soon the two groups had signed a friendship treaty that lasted fifty years.

In the spring of 1621 the *Mayflower* sailed back to England. The Pilgrims watched longingly as the ship sailed away without them, but they had made their choice. This land was their new home, where they would be free to live and worship as they wished.

Plains Indians

The Great Plains cover miles of open rolling country in the middle of the United States. The Indians who lived there were called the Plains Indians.

Before white people came to America few Indians lived on the Great Plains. The ones who did lived near the rivers and streams, where the women grew crops like beans, corn, and squash. The men hunted deer, elk, and sometimes buffalo—but hunting on foot was very difficult.

This way of life changed after the Spanish came to America. The Spanish brought horses with them. When some of these horses went wild, the Indians learned to tame and ride them. Suddenly, hunting the many thousands of buffalo that roamed the Great Plains became much easier.

Before long the Plains Indians' whole life depended on these buffalo. Riding their horses at full speed, the Indian men used their bows and arrows to shoot down the huge buffalo. It took a brave and skillful rider to learn to ride a galloping horse without holding on, and to kill a buffalo with just one arrow!

After the men had killed the buffalo, the women in the

tribe took over. They used up every part of the animal. They roasted the meat over the fire to eat right away, or they sliced and dried it in the sun to eat later. They sewed the skin into clothing, bedding, and tipis and made tools from the bones and horns. They even used the dried buffalo manure, or "chips," to burn instead of wood in their fires!

Now more and more Indians moved to the Great Plains. They never made permanent towns, however, because they always had to follow the herds of buffalo. When it was time to move, they packed up everything— even their huge tipis—and loaded it on sleds pulled by horses. Then the Indian mothers got their babies ready. They wrapped them in buckskin blankets, strapped them to cradleboards, and tied the cradleboards to their backs.

With so many Indians on the Great Plains from so many different tribes, it became important for them to know how to talk to one another. Each tribe had its own spoken language, so the Indians learned to communicate by using sign language.

The Plains Indians had a good life as they followed the buffalo herds. This time was short, though. Soon many white people came to the Great Plains. These people killed most of the buffalo for food or just for fun. Without the buffalo, the way of the Plains Indians could not survive.

The First Thanksgiving

When the Pilgrims landed in Plymouth, Massachusetts, in the winter of 1620, there were ninety-nine men, women, and children in their little band. That first winter was long and cold. Only about half of the Pilgrims lived until spring.

When spring finally came, the Pilgrims who were left set out bravely to make their new homes. They were lucky to have friendly Indians to help them. One man especially taught the Pilgrims many things about their new land. Squanto was his name.

Squanto taught the Pilgrims how to plant corn—four kernels to each hillock. He also showed them how to catch herring from the brook and how to tap maple trees for their sugary sap.

The following summer, life was no longer so cruel. The Pilgrims' crops ripened in the sun. Autumn was beautiful, and the harvest was rich. The Pilgrims were thankful to be alive, so they planned a day of Thanksgiving and a feast.

The Pilgrims went hunting for ducks, geese, and quail. They shot wild turkeys, too, for there were many of them near Plymouth. They also went fishing and brought back many kinds of fish and seafood.

The Indians were invited to the feast, and ninety-one men, women, and children came. They brought five freshly killed deer to share. There was plenty of food for everyone.

Then the Indians and Pilgrims sat down to eat goose and venison, lobster, eel pie, corn, bread, salad, plums, berries, and to drink red and white wine. There were speeches and songs, dances and games. In fact, everyone was having such a good time, no one wanted to leave!

That first Thanksgiving celebration lasted for three days. The Indians went back to their homes, and the Pilgrims prepared for another long, cold winter.

Even today, every year after the harvest in late November, we set aside a day of Thanksgiving to remind us of the Pilgrims and to give thanks for all the good things that are in our country.

Unit Two
Stories and People

Brer Possum and Brer Snake

WILLIAM J. FAULKNER

One frosty morning Brer Possum was going down the road minding his own business, when he came across Brer Snake lying in the road with a brick on his back. Now, Brer Snake is a dangerous creature. He'll bite you if you don't watch out.

So Brer Possum walked around Brer Snake. But then he heard Brer Snake holler out, "Oh, Brer Possum—please, sir—don't leave me here to die. Can't you see the brick on my back? Please lift it off."

Brer Possum looked around, and he looked at Brer Snake, and then he reached down and picked the brick right off Brer Snake's back. And then he went on down the road minding his own business.

But again Brer Snake cried out, "Oh, Brer Possum, don't leave me in the road to die. Don't you see how cold I am? I'm so cold I can't crawl. Pick me up and put me in your pocket, please, sir. You have a warm pocket right there in front."

Brer Possum came back and got Brer Snake and stuck him in his pocket, and then he went on down the road.

All of a sudden Brer Snake stuck his head out of the pocket and said, "I'm going to bite you. I'm going to bite you."

Brer Possum cried, "Why are you going to bite me, Brer Snake? I haven't done anything wrong to you. In fact, I helped you. I lifted the brick off your back, and I stuck you in my pocket."

Brer Snake said, "I don't know. I guess it's just my nature to bite."

Brer Possum sighed. "Well, if I'm going to die, Brer Snake, let me go down to Brer Rabbit's house and tell him good-bye."

"All right," said Brer Snake.

So Brer Possum went down to Brer Rabbit's house. Brer Rabbit was sitting on his front porch, just a-rocking back and forth. He called out, "Hello there, Brer Possum."

"Good morning, Brer Rabbit," answered Brer Possum.

"Where are you going?" asked Brer Rabbit.

Brer Possum said, "I'm not going anywhere. I just came to tell you good-bye because I'm going to die—that's all."

"My goodness, what's the matter with you?" asked Brer Rabbit.

"I've got a snake in my pocket."

"Oh, my!" said Brer Rabbit. "What're you doing with a snake in your pocket? Don't you know he's a dangerous creature?"

"Yes, I know that now, sir."

"Well, what happened?" asked Brer Rabbit.

And then Brer Possum told Brer Rabbit how he had taken the brick off Brer Snake's back and picked him up and stuck him in his pocket, and how Brer Snake had said he was going to bite him.

Brer Rabbit said, "I can't understand that. Is that right, Brer Snake?"

Brer Snake stuck his head out of Brer Possum's pocket and said, "Yes, that's right."

Brer Rabbit shook his head all puzzled-like. "Let's go down where the thing happened, and then maybe I can understand. I can't understand it now."

So the three of them went down the road together. When they reached the brick, Brer Rabbit stepped over beside it, and then he said, "Brer Possum, where were you standing?"

"Right here," answered Brer Possum.

"And, Brer Snake, where were you standing?"

Brer Snake crawled out of Brer Possum's pocket over to the brick and said, "Right here."

Quickly Brer Rabbit slapped the brick down on Brer Snake's back, and jumped away. Then he said, "Now, you just stay there, Brer Snake. That's where poison creatures belong. And you, Brer Possum, don't you ever trouble trouble, until trouble troubles you!"

Our Country's Birthday

The Fourth of July is a very special holiday for the people of the United States. On that day we celebrate our country's birthday. There are parades and picnics, and when night comes, many people gather to watch fireworks light up the sky.

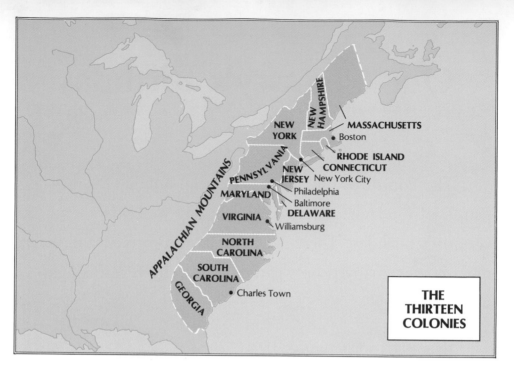

THE
THIRTEEN
COLONIES

Explorers came to our country from many places in Europe. People from countries such as Spain, France, England, and Holland settled here. By the year 1776 there were thirteen English colonies along the east coast. These colonies were ruled by the English king. The people who lived there had to follow English laws and pay taxes to England.

The leaders of the colonies wanted them to be free from England. Many people who lived in the colonies thought the king of England did not care much about them. They were angry because they felt that many of the laws they had to obey were unfair. What made them even angrier were the taxes they had to pay, especially on English goods. If a colonist bought clothing, or tea, or anything that came from England—even newspapers—a special tax was added to the price. That tax money went back to England.

In 1774 and 1775 leaders of these American colonies held meetings in Philadelphia to talk about what to do. They decided that the people didn't need a king to rule them and that the colonies should be free from England. They met again in June of 1776 and decided to send a message to the king declaring their freedom, or independence, from England.

Thomas Jefferson was chosen to write this declaration of independence. He had always believed that people could rule themselves. Jefferson was not a great speaker, but he could say things in writing in such a way that it made people understand and care about his ideas.

Jefferson worked on this task for seventeen days. He wrote and rewrote. His words told the world that America wanted to be free from England.

The words of Thomas Jefferson in the Declaration of Independence are known around the world. He wrote that "all men are created equal." He also said that everyone has the right to "life, liberty, and the pursuit of happiness."

On July 4, 1776, the leaders of the colonies voted to sign their names to the Declaration of Independence. Four days later, the declaration was read to the people of Philadelphia. Bells rang and people cheered. Although they would still have to fight for their freedom, it was on that July day in 1776 that the thirteen American colonies became the United States of America.

Deborah Sampson Goes to War

BRYNA STEVENS

[PART 1]

Deborah Sampson was born on December 17, 1760.

During the first five years of Deborah's life, George Washington worried about pleasing his wife, Martha. Thomas Jefferson worried about getting good grades. Benjamin Franklin worried about politics. The Sampsons worried about money. They never seemed to have enough.

Finally Mr. Sampson decided to become a sailor. Off he went to sea, with high hopes of making enough money to feed his family. But his ship was lost in a storm. His family never saw him again.

There were few jobs for women in the 1760s. Mrs. Sampson could not take care of six children all by herself, so she sent some to live with relatives.

Deborah moved in with her cousin and then with a pastor's widow. Finally, when she was ten years old,

Deborah went to live with the Benjamin Thomas family. This turned out to be a lucky move.

Deborah had to work hard at the Thomas home. She plowed fields and milked cows. She fed animals and made all her own clothes. But she also got to go to school! In 1770 not many girls were that lucky.

Deborah loved school. She especially loved learning to read. Soon she was reading all the newspapers she could find.

What was she reading about? Taxes, for one thing. At that time the United States was made up of thirteen colonies. It wasn't even called the United States yet. All the colonies belonged to Britain.

Britain needed money, so it began to pass new laws. These laws made the colonists pay taxes on many things, like newspapers and tea and paint. The money from these taxes went to Britain.

Many colonists didn't think that was fair at all. Why should their money go to Britain? They were building a new world. They needed their money at home. Britain should leave them alone and let them govern themselves!

These angry colonists were called patriots. Deborah agreed with them.

In 1773 Deborah read about the Boston Tea Party. Some patriots had sneaked onto three British ships. They had thrown 340 chests of British tea into the sea. They were protesting the taxes. Deborah felt they were right.

In 1775 Deborah read the latest news. British soldiers and the patriots had begun to fight against each other. The American Revolution had started.

Deborah wanted to fight too, but she was only fourteen years old. Besides, she was a girl. Only boys and men were allowed to join the army.

Seven years later Deborah was twenty-one, and the war was still going on. Deborah was now a tall young woman. In fact, she was taller than many men. She was strong too.

If men can fight for freedom, Deborah wondered, why

can't I? The more she thought about it, the more she wanted to fight.

So one day Deborah made a man's suit. She tied her hair back the way men did. She put on her new suit. Then she walked thirty-five miles to Billingham, Massachusetts. There she joined the army.

No one in Billingham knew Deborah. She signed her name Robert Shurtleff. No one guessed that she was a woman. She joined a regiment at West Point, near New York City.

[PART 2]

Fighting was hard around New York City. The British were stealing cows from American farmers. The cows became food for the British army. Deborah's regiment was told to put a stop to this stealing.

During the battle a bullet hit Deborah's head. "Don't take me to a hospital," she begged. "Just let me die!"

Of course the soldiers refused to obey her. Instead, a soldier put her on his horse. He rode six miles to a hospital.

Deborah was badly hurt, but she was afraid of the hospital more than she was afraid of pain. She was sure that someone would find out that she was a woman. She was so worried that she left the hospital before she was completely well.

Luckily her next job was easy. She went to work for General Paterson in his home. Then, a few months later, she was sent to Philadelphia.

American soldiers were supposed to be paid $6.67 a month, but Congress had no money to pay them. Most of the soldiers went on fighting without pay. Some refused to fight. Instead, they took over the State House. Deborah was sent to Philadelphia with 1,500 other soldiers to quiet the angry men.

Winter came. Deborah's shoes were worn out. The army didn't give clothes to soldiers. They had to buy their own. Deborah didn't have enough money to buy new shoes. Her bloody feet left red stains in the snow. Soon she became ill.

Once more, soldiers took her to a hospital. This time Deborah slept for days. The doctors thought she was dead.

She could hear people planning to bury her, but she was too weak to cry out. When a nurse passed by, Deborah tried to groan. The nurse heard her and ran for help.

Dr. Binney came and began to examine Deborah. He stared in surprise. There was no doubt about it. Private Shurtleff was a woman!

Dr. Binney kept Deborah's secret. When she was well, Deborah went back to her regiment.

The Revolutionary War was coming to an end. In 1783 Deborah was called to West Point. Peace had been made. The Americans had won! Deborah's regiment was no longer needed.

When she got to West Point, General Paterson sent for Deborah. He looked at a letter on his desk. The letter was from Dr. Binney.

General Paterson laughed. There *couldn't* be a woman in *my* army, he thought.

The general showed the letter to Deborah. He thought that she would laugh too. Instead, her face turned red.

General Paterson stared at her. "Private Shurtleff," he said, "I must ask this question. Are you a woman?"

"Yes, sir," Deborah answered. "I am. My real name is Deborah Sampson."

My First Buffalo Hunt

CHIEF STANDING BEAR

[PART 1]

I had learned to make arrows and tip them with feathers. I knew how to ride my pony, no matter how fast he would go, and I felt I was brave and did not fear danger. All these things I had learned for just this day when Father would allow me to go with him on a buffalo hunt. It was the day for which every Sioux boy eagerly waited. To ride side by side with the best hunters of the tribe, to hear the terrible noise of the great herds as they ran, and then to help bring home the kill made this the most thrilling day of any Indian boy's life.

We all knew that the scouts had come in and reported buffalo near and that we must all keep the camp in stillness. Even the horses and dogs were quiet, and all night not a horse neighed and not a dog barked. Quiet was everywhere.

The night before a buffalo hunt was always an exciting night, even though it was quiet in camp. There would be much talk in the tipis around the fires. There would be

46

sharpening of arrows and of knives. New bowstrings would be made, and quivers would be filled with arrows.

It was in the fall of the year, and the evenings were cool as Father and I sat by the fire and talked over the hunt. I was only eight years of age, and I knew that my father did not expect me to get a buffalo at all, but only to try perhaps for a small calf should I be able to get close enough to one. I was greatly excited as I sat and watched Father working in his easy, firm way.

You can picture me, I think, as I sat in the glow of the campfire, my little brown body bare to the waist, watching, listening to my father. My hair hung down my back, and I wore moccasins and a breechcloth of buckskin. To my belt was fastened a rawhide holster for my knife, and this night, I remember, I kept it on all night. I went to sleep with my bow in hand to be all the nearer ready in the morning when the start was made.

The next morning the leaders went ahead until they saw the herd of grazing buffalo. Then they stopped and waited for the rest of us to ride up. We all rode slowly up to the herd, which had come together as soon as they saw us. They ran close together, all of them, as if at the command of a leader. We continued riding slowly toward the herd until one of the leaders shouted, "Ho-ka-he!" which means "Ready, go!" At that command every man started for the herd. I had been listening too, and the minute the hunters started, I rode with them.

Away I went, my little pony putting all he had into the race. It was not long before I lost sight of Father, but I kept going just the same. I threw my blanket back, and the chill of the autumn morning struck my body, but I did not mind.

On I went. It was wonderful to race over the ground with all these horsemen about me. There was no shouting, no noise of any kind except the pounding of horses' feet. The herd was now running and had raised a cloud of dust. I felt no fear until we had entered this cloud of dust and I could see nothing about me—I could only hear the sound of feet. Where was Father? Where was I going? On I rode through the cloud, for I knew I must keep going.

[PART 2]

All at once I saw that I was in the midst of the buffalo. Their dark bodies were rushing all about me, and their great heads were moving up and down to the sound of their hoofs

49

beating upon the earth. Then I was afraid, and I leaned close down upon my little pony's body and clutched him tightly. I can never tell you how I felt toward my pony at that moment. All thought of shooting had left my mind. I was filled with fear. In a moment or so, my senses became clearer and I could hear other sounds besides the clatter of feet. I could hear a shot now and then, and I could see the buffalo beginning to break up into small bunches. I could not see my father or any of the others yet, but I was not so frightened any more.

I let my pony run. The buffalo looked too large for me to tackle anyway, so I just kept going. The buffalo became more and more scattered. Pretty soon I saw a young calf that looked about my size. I remembered now what Father had told me the night before as we sat about the fire. Those instructions were important for me to follow now. I wanted to try for that young buffalo calf.

I was still back of the calf, unable to get alongside of him. I was eager to get a shot yet afraid to try. I was still very nervous. While my pony was making all speed to come alongside, I tried a shot, and to my surprise my arrow landed. My second arrow glanced along the back of the animal and sped on between the horns, making only a slight wound.

My third arrow hit a spot that made the running beast
slow up. I shot a fourth arrow, and though it, too, landed, it
was not a fatal wound. It seemed to me that it was taking a
lot of shots, and I was not proud of my marksmanship. I
was glad, however, to see the animal going slower, and I
knew that one more shot would make me a hunter. My
horse seemed to know his own importance. His ears stood
straight forward, and it was not necessary for me to urge
him to get closer to the buffalo.

I was soon by the side of the buffalo, and one more
shot brought the chase to an end. I jumped from my pony
and stood by my fallen buffalo. I looked all around wishing
that the world could see. But I was alone.

I was wondering what to do when I heard my father's
voice calling, "To-ki-i-la-la-hu-wo?" ["Where are you?"] I

quickly jumped on my pony and rode to the top of a little hill nearby. Father saw me and came to me at once. He was so pleased to see me and glad to know that I was safe. As he came up, I said as calmly as I could, "Father, I have killed a buffalo." His smile changed to surprise, and he asked me where my buffalo was. I pointed to it, and we rode over to where it lay.

Father set to work to skin it for me. I had watched him do this many times and knew perfectly well how to do it myself, but I could not turn the animal over. When the hide was off, Father put it on the pony's back with the hair side next to the pony. On this he arranged the meat so it would balance. Then he covered the meat carefully with the rest of the hide so no dust would reach it while we traveled home.

Always when arriving home I would run out to play, for I loved to be with the other boys. But this day I stayed close to the tipi so I could hear the nice things that were said about me. It was soon all over camp that I had killed a buffalo.

My father was so proud that he gave away a fine horse. He called an old man to our tipi to cry out the news to the rest of the people in camp.

That ended my first and last buffalo hunt. It lives only in my memory, for the last days of the buffalo are over.

Buffalo Dusk

CARL SANDBURG

The buffaloes are gone.
And those who saw the buffaloes are gone.
Those who saw the buffaloes by thousands and how
    they pawed the prairie sod into dust with their
    hoofs, their great heads down pawing on in a
    great pageant of dusk,
Those who saw the buffaloes are gone.
And the buffaloes are gone.

Lysbet and the Fire Kittens

MARIETTA MOSKIN

It was December 1662 in the small Dutch colony of New Amsterdam. Lysbet's sister, Nellie, was having a baby. Ma, who had gone to help her, had left Lysbet in charge of the house. Lysbet was glad to be taking care of everything. Stuyver, the cat, was most important because she was going to have kittens.

Pa and Dirk were trading on the Hudson River. They had trouble with their boat and didn't get home, so Lysbet spent the night alone.

Things started to go wrong in the morning, when Lysbet saw that she had let the fire go out. She worked hard to get a new fire started and then did chores all morning. At last all her work was done. Surely Ma wouldn't want her to stay home any longer! She took her brand-new skates and went to the pond to skate. It was fun to be skating with the other children at last.

As Lysbet glided across the ice, something kept nagging at the back of her mind. She hadn't forgotten anything, had she? She had built a big fire that would not go out. The

floor had been swept, the dishes cleared. The pigs and the chickens had been fed.

The animals! The cat! She had forgotten to feed Stuyver. Just now Stuyver needed extra food because she was expecting her kittens.

Lysbet took off her skates. Back home she ran, her striped petticoats flashing.

"Stuyver," Lysbet called as she tumbled into the house. "I'm sorry, Stuyver, where are you?"

There was no sign of the cat in the house. But there was something else—a strange smell. It was smoke—thick, heavy smoke.

"Fire!" Lysbet cried. "Fire!" She stood still with horror. A fire was a terrible thing, the worst thing that could happen in a town of wooden houses thatched with straw. What should she do? She must give the alarm. The whole town might burn down if the fire spread!

Lysbet tore the leather fire bucket from its hook by the door. She tossed it into the street. That way the fire fighters could use it while she ran to spread the alarm.

"Fire!" Lysbet called, running down Pearl Street.

Doors and windows opened. From everywhere leather fire buckets bounced and tumbled into the streets. Men, women, and children ran from their homes. They grabbed up the buckets and ran to the river to start a bucket brigade.

Near Stone Street, someone took up Lysbet's cry. It was Lodewyk Pos, captain of the rattle watch, the town fire brigade. The watchman shook his loud rattle. "Fire on Pearl Street!" he shouted.

Now Lysbet could go back and look for Stuyver. She rushed home and stood in front of the house.

"Please, Stuyver, come out," Lysbet cried. How could Stuyver find her way out in all that smoke?

"Stuyver! Come! Hurry!" Lysbet was close to tears. She couldn't see any flames, but the smoke hurt her eyes. The house isn't safe, Lysbet thought. Stuyver's got to come out.

Then she heard a sound—a mewing. Stuyver! Stuyver was at the door. She was pulling at something. Kittens! Stuyver had had her litter of kittens by the door. Lysbet bent down, scooping the kittens into her apron. One, two, three, four, five, she counted—five tiny, wriggling balls of fur.

Her eyes streaming with tears, Lysbet dashed away from the house with Stuyver close at her heels.

She leaned against the gatepost as she caught her breath. Now she could see the flames, bright orange flames, licking at the roof thatch around the chimney.

Many people were struggling to save Lysbet's house. They were trying to keep the flames from spreading farther, from burning up the whole town. The men heaved and hauled the full, heavy buckets from the river to the house. Next to them, the women and children threw the empty ones back down the line. Lysbet watched other neighbors carrying furniture from the house. There was Pa's chair and Ma's spinning wheel.

Lysbet turned away. How could she look, when Ma had left her in charge of the house, when Ma had told her to watch the fire, but she had gone skating instead? Now Ma and Pa would come home to a ruined house, with nothing left but odds and ends and an apronful of new kittens.

Then someone was calling her name. It was Pa, and behind him was Dirk. "Lysbet, Lysbet," Pa said. "Thank God you are well."

Lysbet felt Pa's strong arm around her. "I'm sorry," she sobbed.

"Sorry?" Pa asked. "You saved our house! You gave the alarm before it went up in flames."

"But it was all my fault," Lysbet cried. Snuggling even closer against Pa, she sobbed out the whole story.

Pa shook his head. Babies and kittens and fires, all in one day! That was too much. Poor Lysbet. "I must teach you to lay a safe fire," he said, "not a fire so big that the sparks fly up through the flue."

Now Lysbet knew how the fire had started. Sparks from the chimney had rained down on the roof and set it ablaze.

"But we were lucky," Pa said. "The roof was so wet from the snow that the fire could only smolder. And I guess we were lucky, too, that you forgot Stuyver's milk!"

Lysbet looked up at Pa. She hugged him tight. He led Lysbet inside. The room was a mess. It was full of water and soot. Pa took Lysbet's hand. "It will take lots of hard work," he said. "But we'll have it clean enough before Ma comes home."

Lysbet knelt down by Stuyver, who was busy washing her kittens. "You saved your babies," she told Stuyver. "I'll help you take care of them."

The big cat only purred in reply.

The Legend of the Bluebonnet

Retold by TOMIE dePAOLA

"Great Spirits, the land is dying. Your People are dying, too," the long line of dancers sang. "Tell us what we have done to anger you. End this drought. Save your People. Tell us what we must do so you will send the rain that will bring back life."

For three days the dancers danced to the sound of the drums, and for three days the People watched and waited. And even though the hard winter was over, no healing rains came.

Drought and famine are hardest on the very young and the very old. Among the few children left was a small girl named She-Who-Is-Alone. She sat by herself watching the dancers. In her lap was a doll made from buckskin—a warrior doll. The eyes, nose, and mouth were painted on with the juice of berries. It wore beaded leggings and a belt of polished bone. On its head were brilliant blue feathers from the bird who cries "Jay-jay-jay." She loved her doll very much.

"Soon," She-Who-Is-Alone said to her doll, "the shaman will go off alone to the top of the hill to listen for the words of the Great Spirits. Then we will know what to do so that once more the rains will come and the Earth will be green and alive. The buffalo will be plentiful, and the People will be rich again."

As she talked, she thought of the mother who made the doll, of the father who brought the blue feathers. She thought of the grandfather and the grandmother she had never known. They were all like shadows. It seemed long ago that they had died from the famine. The People had named her and cared for her. The warrior doll was the only thing she had left from those distant days.

"The sun is setting," the runner called as he ran through the camp. "The shaman is returning." The People gathered in a circle and the shaman spoke.

"I have heard the words of the Great Spirits," he said. "The People have become selfish. For years, they have taken from the Earth without giving anything back. The Great Spirits say the People must sacrifice. We must make a burnt offering of the most valued possession among us. The ashes of this offering shall then be scattered to the four points of the Earth, the Home of the Winds. When this sacrifice is made, drought and famine will cease. Life will be restored to the Earth and to the People!"

The People sang a song of thanks to the Great Spirits for telling them what they must do.

"I'm sure it is not my new bow that the Great Spirits want," a warrior said. "Or my special blanket," a woman added, as everyone went to their tipis to talk and think over what the Great Spirits had asked.

Everyone, that is, except She-Who-Is-Alone. She held her doll tightly to her heart. "You," she said, looking at the doll, "you are my most valued possession. It is you the Great Spirits want." And she knew what she must do.

As the council fires died out and the tipi flaps began to close, the small girl returned to the tipi where she slept to wait.

The night outside was still except for the distant sound of the night bird with the red wings. Soon everyone in the tipi was asleep, except She-Who-Is-Alone. Under the ashes of the tipi fire one stick still glowed. She took it and quietly crept out into the night.

She ran to the place on the hill where the Great Spirits had spoken to the shaman. Stars filled the sky, but there was no moon. "O Great Spirits," She-Who-Is-Alone said, "here is my warrior doll. It is the only thing I have from my family who died in this famine. It is my most valued possession. Please accept it."

Then, gathering twigs, she started a fire with the glowing firestick. The small girl watched as the twigs began to catch and burn. She thought of her grandmother and grandfather, her mother and father, and all the People— their suffering, their hunger. And before she could change her mind, she thrust the doll into the fire.

64

She watched until the flames died down and the ashes
had grown cold. Then, scooping up a handful, She-Who-Is-
Alone scattered the ashes to the Home of the Winds, the
North and the East, the South and the West. And then she
fell asleep until the first light of the morning sun woke her.

She looked out over the hill, and stretching out from all sides, where the ashes had fallen, the ground was covered with flowers—beautiful flowers, as blue as the feathers in the hair of the doll, as blue as the feathers of the bird who cries, "Jay-jay-jay."

When the People came out of their tipis, they could scarcely believe their eyes. They gathered on the hill with She-Who-Is-Alone to look at the miraculous sight. There was no doubt about it—the flowers were a sign of forgiveness from the Great Spirits.

As the People sang and danced their thanks to the Great Spirits, a warm rain began to fall, and the land began to live again. From that day on, the little girl was known by another name—"One-Who-Dearly-Loved-Her-People."

Every spring, the Great Spirits remember the sacrifice of a little girl and fill the hills and valleys of the land, now called Texas, with the beautiful blue flowers.

Even to this very day.

Unit Three
Our Country Grows

The Spanish in California

ABIGAIL KELLEY

For a long time the Spanish were the only white people in North America. They lived in Mexico, which was then called New Spain.

Soon after they came to America the Spanish began exploring the land to the north of Mexico. In 1542 some explorers sailed up the Pacific Coast. They found a safe harbor and a land they named California. Another explorer sailed north again about 60 years later. Then the Spanish forgot California for more than 160 years.

By the middle 1700s Spanish lands stretched from Florida and Louisiana in the east, across Texas, to New

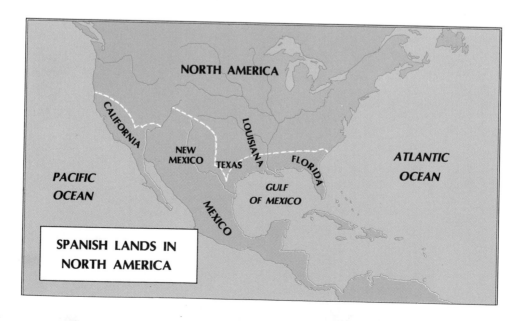

SPANISH LANDS IN NORTH AMERICA

Mexico in the west. The Spanish built missions, forts, mining camps, ranches, and towns on these lands.

About this time English and Russian explorers began coming to the Pacific Coast. The Spaniards once more became interested in California because they were afraid they might lose the land they had claimed. To keep it they planned to build missions among the Indians and forts to protect the missions.

Father Junipero Serra was sent from Mexico to start the missions. The first one was built at San Diego. By 1823 there were twenty-one missions along the coast of California.

Each mission was like a town with a wall around it. It had houses, workshops, kitchens, storerooms, and barns. The most important building was the church. Outside the walls were the fields and orchards that belonged to the mission. Crops were grown on this land, and large herds of cattle and sheep grazed there.

Many missions thrived because they owned so much land and because Indians did much of the work. Mission life was not always easy for the Indians, who had to learn new ways and work very hard.

Then other people from Mexico wanted to settle in California. Bit by bit, mission lands were sold to new settlers or given to soldiers when they retired from the army. These large pieces of land were called *ranchos*. Some *ranchos* stretched as far as the eye could see and had many horses

and great herds of cattle. California became an important center for cattle raising.

Before long, American settlers began coming to California. Soon many Americans were there. They wanted California to become part of the United States. This finally happened when the United States won the Mexican War.

That same year gold was discovered in northern California. People poured into California from all parts of the world. Some found gold, but many of those who didn't stayed to become farmers and ranchers and to start new towns and businesses. On 9 September 1850 California became the thirty-first state in the Union.

Westward Ho!

MABEL HARMER

About a hundred and fifty years after the Pilgrims had settled in this country, a young hunter picked up his gun. He tossed it onto his shoulder and followed a buffalo trail across the mountains into what is now Kentucky. His name was Daniel Boone.

Daniel Boone found wild country west of the mountains. There were no settlers and no roads. Indians hunted in the woods for food. The country was beautiful but dangerous. Here was rich, free land, thought Daniel Boone—miles and miles of it.

Many settlers besides the Pilgrims had come to America. They had stayed on the safe land between the Atlantic Ocean and the mountains.

Daniel Boone came back and told people about the wild country beyond the mountains. He told about the dangers and the mysteries of the forests. He told about the miles and miles of rich land that had never been plowed.

People listened. A few of them wanted to go across the mountains to make new homes. It would mean danger and excitement and adventure, and a chance to get good, rich land. Daniel Boone led a small group of these pioneers across the mountains.

Fur traders, men searching for gold, and hunters like Daniel Boone had already seen this wild country. Indians had lived there for many years, but the pioneers led by Boone were the first white people to go to build their homes in the new land. For a hundred years after Daniel Boone showed a way across the mountains, American pioneers moved westward toward the Pacific Ocean. Some pioneers

traveled on foot. Some rode horses or mules. But most of
the families used covered wagons.

Wagon wheels were wide for rolling over soft earth.
Wagon ends were high so that things inside would not slide
out on the hills. The wagons were loaded with flour, salt,
cornmeal, bedding, tools, and a few pieces of furniture.
There would be no stores where the pioneers were going.

Most of the wagons were pulled by oxen. Oxen were
slow, but they were strong.

It wasn't easy traveling by wagon. Sometimes trees had to be cut down to clear a path. A wagon wheel might hit a rock and break. Heavy rains made great mud holes, and wagons often got stuck. Uphill travel was hard, and downhill travel was dangerous. Strong men tied ropes to the wagons and hung onto them to keep the wagons from tumbling end over end down the hill.

The oxen could pull the wagons across small streams, but there were deep rivers to cross, too. Then logs were tied to the wheels to keep the wagons afloat. The oxen swam and pulled the wagons across, while men on swimming horses helped to guide them.

Sometimes a wagon broke loose and turned over in the water. Then the pioneers had to try to save whatever they could.

There were times when the pioneers and their wagons could move down a river on a flatboat. This was a much easier way to travel.

But no matter how they traveled, the pioneers could go only a few miles in a day. After months of traveling, they finally reached the lands they had heard so much about. They built houses and began towns. They had opened up the way to the West and helped this country grow to become what it is today.

Open Range

KATHRYN and BYRON JACKSON

Prairie goes to the mountain,
   Mountain goes to the sky.
The sky sweeps across to the distant hills
And here, in the middle,
   Am I.

Hills crowd down to the river,
   River runs by the tree.
Tree throws its shadow on sunburnt grass
And here, in the shadow,
   Is me.

Shadows creep up the mountain,
   Mountain goes black on the sky.
The sky bursts out with a million stars
And here, by the campfire,
   Am I.

Journey for Sacajawea

JOHANNA JOHNSTON

[PART 1]

Was it possible? Was she really going to see the Shining Mountains again? Sacajawea could hardly believe it. She had been a child when the Hidatsa people had stolen her away from the mountain country of her own people, the Shoshonis. Through the years, the wandering Hidatsa had taken her farther and farther east. She was a young woman now, married to a French-Canadian trapper named Charbonneau. It was he, her husband, who was saying that she would see the mountains again. He told her how and why.

A group of explorers from even farther to the east had come to Fort Mandan, where Sacajawea and her husband lived. The explorers were going west. They had been sent by President Thomas Jefferson to explore the Northwest. They were also looking for a water route to the Pacific Ocean.

Two young captains, Captain Lewis and Captain Clark, were leading the group. They wanted a guide. Sacajawea's husband had said that he would take the job.

When Lewis and Clark heard that Sacajawea was a Shoshoni, they asked her to teach them her language. They wanted her to come with them and help them talk to the Shoshonis. "Our journey is going to be a hard one," they said.

Sacajawea's husband replied, "She is strong. Besides, she will help you get horses from her people to travel over the mountains."

And so it was settled. Sacajawea would go with her

husband on the long journey with Lewis and Clark. With her also would go her baby boy.

When spring came, the group set off in dugout canoes to follow the Missouri River westward. Sacajawea sat in one of the canoes with her baby on her back in a cradleboard. Secretly, she wondered what kind of journey these Americans were making. Her husband had told her that the Americans had bought many miles of the country from France. These men just wanted to explore it. Sacajawea saw that they had many guns with them. If she helped lead them to her people, would they do the Shoshonis harm?

Day after day they traveled, and Sacajawea watched and listened. Every night, the two captains wrote in journals, making notes on what they had seen that day, for this country had never been seen by white people before.

[PART 2]

Every day there was a new adventure. Once they were frightened by a grizzly bear. One day there was a storm, and the main canoe almost turned over. Maps and the captains' journals floated off into the water. Sacajawea reached out and collected the papers. The captains were very grateful to her. Sacajawea was happy that she had been able to help. She had begun to like and trust the Americans. She was also able to help them by finding plants that were safe to eat. These plants helped everyone stay well.

The river narrowed, and the hills grew higher. Sometimes they had to leave the water and climb on land, carrying the canoes. Higher they went, and higher, until at last they came to a pass. Ahead they saw the snowy peaks of the Rocky Mountains—Sacajawea's Shining Mountains. Sacajawea stood very still, just looking. Then she took her baby from her back and held him so that he too could see the mountains.

They were very near Shoshoni country now. Sacajawea taught the captains some Shoshoni words and friendly signs to help them when they met her people. She wondered if anyone who had known her when she was a little girl would still be with the tribe. She was sure her older brother had been killed in the long-ago attack when she had been stolen away.

The day came when they met the Shoshonis, galloping up on the horses that were their pride. Years before, Spaniards had brought horses to Mexico, and some had escaped to the plains and become wild. The Shoshonis, like other western Indians, had caught some and tamed them. Now they could not think how they had hunted buffalo without horses.

Captain Lewis and Captain Clark greeted the Shoshoni chief with the words Sacajawea had taught them. Then they called Sacajawea to tell them what the chief was saying.

Sacajawea came and looked up at the chief. She could hardly believe what she saw. The chief was her own brother. "Cameahwait [Little Bear]!" she cried.

"Sacajawea [Bird Girl]!" he said, and they put their arms around one another.

Now, with Sacajawea's help, it was easy for the Americans to buy horses from the Shoshonis for the journey over the Rocky Mountains. The journey went on. Up, up, up they went, to what seemed the top of the world, and then down again. Then they went across more miles, until they came to the Columbia River. Here they left the horses and took to boats again.

They traveled more miles, past rapids and rocks. Finally, on a day of blowing rain and fog, they saw ahead the waters of the Pacific Ocean. For the first time white people had crossed the whole continent of America.

They spent the winter by the ocean. In the spring they began the long journey home. When they got back to Fort Mandan, it was time for Sacajawea and her husband to say good-bye to the explorers.

Sacajawea was sad as she parted from Lewis and Clark. Many white people had brought fear and trouble to the Indian people in the past. Many more would do so in the future. But Sacajawea had known something better—a wonderful journey and strangers who had become friends.

The Great Pacific Railroad

When the United States was first a country, many
people from all over the world wanted to come to live in the
American West. Few, however, could stand the hardships
and dangers of travel by horseback and covered wagon.
Americans began to talk of building a railroad across the
country, from the Atlantic Ocean all the way to the Pacific.

The first railroads were horse-drawn wagons running
on wooden rails. A man would set his wagon on the rails,
then hitch up his horse and start off. The wooden rails made
a smooth road. Still, this was a hard, slow way to travel.

Then all of this was changed by the invention of the steam-powered locomotive—the "Iron Horse." The Iron Horse made travel much easier and faster. It would also make the dream of a railroad all the way to the Pacific Ocean come true.

It was the time of the Civil War between the Northern and Southern states. The United States government needed a

railroad to ship war goods and household supplies. It could
not build a railroad and fight a war at the same time,
though, so it gave land to two railroad companies. The
Union Pacific company was to build westward from Omaha,
Nebraska. The Central Pacific company was to build
eastward from Sacramento, California. Each railroad
company was to build until the two lines met.

To lay the iron rails for the steam locomotive, a level
road had to be built. Some people said a railroad couldn't
be built through the desert. Others said it couldn't be built
through the mountains. But the railroad builders blasted and
dug through both mountains and deserts. They lived
through buffalo stampedes and landslides. They brought
their equipment to California from New York by sea. Ships
sailed all the way around the tip of South America. Whatever
it took, they did! And they did it all in a shorter time than
anyone had thought possible—less than seven years.

The people who built the railroad were mostly
newcomers to America. They poured strength and spirit into
their new land. They learned to love it and made it their
own. The westbound tracks were laid by Irish immigrants,

88

former slaves, and Civil War veterans. The eastbound tracks were laid by some five thousand Chinese workers.

The Irish came to Omaha to work for the Union Pacific. They dug their way across the prairie like terriers digging for bones. "Tarriers" they called themselves, in the accent of their native land. Part of the tarriers' job was fighting off the Indians, who had been pushed farther and farther west by the settlers. They did not want to be driven out again. They did everything they could to stop the Iron Horse from coming in and spoiling their hunting grounds.

At the same time out in the West, the Chinese had come to work for the Central Pacific. The task ahead of them was to build the railroad across the snowclad Sierra Nevada Mountains. This they did, working only with saws and picks and shovels and charges of dynamite. Sometimes they worked while hanging over the mountainside in baskets. Sometimes they tunneled through mountains in the dead of winter. Many workers died in falls and landslides.

As the two lines drew closer and closer together, the Irish and the Chinese began to race to see who could lay the most track. Newspapers reported the race, and people bet

on the outcome. Finally, on May 10, 1869, the two lines were joined in Promontory, Utah. The last spike, made of gold, was driven in with a silver hammer. The Great Pacific Railroad was open for business. It was a great day for America!

Thanks to the Great Pacific Railroad, the American West lay wide open for people to explore and settle. People now knew that much of the land they had thought unfit to live on was really fine farmland. New settlers came from all over Europe to homestead in what would become the great wheat and corn areas of our country. Big industrial towns grew up, using the railroad to ship their freight. These changes and many others came about because of the brave workers who laid eighteen hundred miles of track through a wilderness. They made it possible to cross America by rail, from sea to shining sea.

Drill, Ye Tarriers

RAILROAD WORK SONG

Ev'ry mornin' at seven o'clock,
There were twenty tarriers a-drillin' on the rock,
And the boss comes around, and he says, "Keep still!
Come down heavy on the cast iron drill;
And drill, ye Tarriers, drill!
And drill, ye Tarriers, drill!
For it's work all day for sugar in your tay,
Down behind the railway,
And drill, ye Tarriers, drill!"

I'd Like to Be a Lighthouse

RACHEL FIELD

I'd like to be a lighthouse
  All scrubbed and painted white.
I'd like to be a lighthouse
  And stay awake all night
To keep my eye on everything
  That sails my patch of sea;
I'd like to be a lighthouse
  With the ships all watching me.

Foghorns

LILIAN MOORE

The foghorns moaned
  in the bay last night
so sad
so deep
I thought I heard the city
  crying in its sleep.

92

Annie Sullivan and Helen Keller

MARY MALONE

Captain and Mrs. Keller of Tuscumbia, Alabama, needed a teacher for their little girl, Helen. Helen was six years old—and had been blind, deaf, and mute since before she was two. The Kellers wrote to the Perkins Institution, a school for the blind in Boston. The school sent a young woman named Annie Sullivan to be Helen's teacher. Annie had been nearly blind when she was little. Then she had some operations on her eyes. She could see now, but she knew what it would be like to be blind.

[PART 1]

Annie got to Tuscumbia after a long, dusty train ride. She was tired, and her eyes were sore from the cinders and

coal dust. Captain and Mrs. Keller met her at the station. They were very glad to see her. They had been meeting every train for two days.

Helen was waiting at the Kellers' house. She sensed that something different was happening. Annie saw how lost and unhappy the child looked. She hoped with all her heart that she could bring Helen Keller out of the darkness.

Annie soon saw that Helen had had no training at all. Her family felt sorry for her and let her do just as she pleased. Helen grabbed anything she wanted, even food from other people's plates. Annie felt sorry for Helen too, but she meant to treat her like any other person.

At her first meal with the family, Annie sat beside Helen. She stopped the little girl from taking other people's food and stuffing it into her mouth. First Helen was surprised. Then she became angry and stamped her feet. Annie asked the family to leave the room. She locked the door after them so Helen would not run away.

Helen kicked the door and struck out at Annie. She screamed and rolled on the floor. Annie forced her to sit down and eat from her own plate, using a spoon and a napkin. It took hours before Helen obeyed. Annie was worn out. She let Helen go, then went to her room, threw herself on the bed, and cried.

After a while Annie began to feel better. She had an idea. She would take Helen away from her family. Helen would have to get used to being alone with Annie and doing as Annie said.

The next day Annie asked Captain Keller if she and Helen could live by themselves for a while. Captain Keller did not like this idea, but Annie said it was the only way to control Helen. At last he agreed.

Annie took Helen to a little cottage not far away from the big house. Her plan started off badly. Helen would not let Annie touch her all day. She fought when Annie tried to put her to bed that night. At last, tired out, Helen fell asleep.

In the morning, Annie gave Helen her clothes to put on. Helen threw them down. Annie would not give Helen breakfast until she was dressed.

For several days it went like this. Helen was strong and stubborn, but Annie was a little stronger and just as stubborn.

One morning Captain Keller came by and looked in the window. He saw Helen sitting on the floor in her nightgown. Annie knew he was angry. She heard from a servant that he wanted to send her back to Boston. But Annie stuck to her plan. She knew she must control Helen before she could teach her.

[PART 2]

Annie kept trying to teach Helen language. Since Helen could not hear words, she had to be taught finger spelling. And since she could not see, she had to feel the words with her hands. Annie used a finger alphabet to spell words into Helen's hands. Helen learned finger spelling quickly. But she

did not yet understand that everything has a name and that words stand for these names. She did not know that thoughts can be put into words and that words can be put together to form sentences.

At last Helen began to behave better. Annie wrote in her diary that Helen was no longer so wild. Annie could touch her, even hold her on her lap.

After two weeks Annie and Helen went back to the big house. The Kellers were very pleased to see the change in

96

Helen. Now she would sit quietly and play with her dolls. Annie taught the family the finger alphabet so that they could talk with Helen.

It was spring and very beautiful in Alabama. Annie kept Helen out of doors most of the time. They went to see the farm animals and took long walks in the woods. Annie taught Helen to know many things by touching and smelling them. Her fingers kept tapping the words for them into Helen's hand. Sometimes Helen got words and objects mixed up.

She was mixed up about *mug* and *water*. Annie thought of a way to make it clear. She took Helen to the outdoor water pump and had her hold a mug while water was pumped into it. The cold water gushed out and spilled over Helen's hand. Annie spelled *water* as this happened.

Suddenly Helen's face changed. She looked alive at last. She spelled *water* by herself many times. She pointed to the pump, then to the ground, and asked for names. Quickly Annie spelled words into Helen's hand.

Helen wanted to know the name of every object she touched. She learned thirty new words in a very short time. Annie was overjoyed. She knew that she had broken through the darkness at last. She had given Helen a key to the world around her—the key of language.

Then Helen asked for Annie's name. Annie spelled *Teacher*. Always, from then on, this was Helen's name for Annie.

That night Helen hugged Annie and kissed her. Annie's heart was full of happiness. She knew that Helen loved her. She knew that she wanted to spend her life helping Helen.

The Dugout

BARBARA BRENNER

"There it is, boys," Daddy said. "Across this river is
Nicodemus, Kansas. That's where we're going to build our
house. There is free land for everyone here in the West. All
we have to do is go and get it."

We had come a long way to get to Kansas—all the way
from Kentucky. It had been a hard trip and a sad one.
Mama died on the way. Now there were just the four of
us—Daddy, Willie, Little Brother, and me.

"Come on, boys," Daddy called. "Let's put our feet on free dirt."

We crossed the river, wagon and all. A man was waiting for us on the other side.

"I am Sam Hickman," he said. "Welcome to the town of Nicodemus."

"Why, thank you, Brother," Daddy said. "But where *is* your town?"

"Right here," Mr. Hickman said.

We did not see any houses. We saw smoke coming out of holes in the prairie.

"Shucks!" Daddy said. "Holes in the ground are for rabbits and snakes, not for free black people. I am a carpenter. I can build fine wood houses for this town."

"No time to build wood houses now," Mr. Hickman told Daddy. "Winter is coming—and winter in Kansas is *mean*. Better get yourself a dugout before the ground freezes."

Daddy knew Sam Hickman was right. We got our shovels, and we dug us a dugout.

It wasn't much of a place—dirt floor, dirt walls, no windows. The roof was just grass and branches. But we were glad to have that dugout when the wind began to whistle across the prairie.

Every night Willie lit the lamp and made a fire. I cooked a rabbit stew or fried a pan of fish fresh from the river. After supper Daddy would always say, "How about a song or two?" He would take out his banjo and *Plink-a-plunk! Plink-a-plunk!* Pretty soon that dugout felt like home.

Winter came. That Kansas winter *was* mean. It snowed day after day. We could not hunt or fish. We had no more rabbit stew and no more fish fresh from the river. All we had to eat was cornmeal mush.

Then one day there was no more cornmeal. There was not a lick of food in the whole town of Nicodemus. And there was nothing left to burn for firewood. Little Brother cried all the time because he was so cold and hungry. Daddy wrapped blankets around him.

"Hush, baby son," he said to him. "Try to sleep. Supply train will be coming soon."

But the supply train did not come—not that day or the next.

On the third day we heard the sound of horses. Daddy looked out to see who it was.

"Oh, no!" he said. "Indians!"

We were *so* scared. We had all heard stories about Indians. I tried to be brave. "I will get my gun, Daddy," I said.

But Daddy said, "Hold on, Johnny. Wait and see what they do."

We watched from the dugout. Everyone in Nicodemus was watching the Indians. First they made a circle. Then each Indian took something from his saddlebag and dropped it on the ground. The Indians turned and rode straight toward the dugouts.

"Now they are coming for us!" Willie cried.

We raised our guns. The Indians rode right past us and kept on going. We waited a long time to be sure they were gone. Then everyone ran out into the snow to see what the Indians had left. It was *food!*

Everyone talked at once.

"Look!"

"Fresh deer meat!"

"Fish!"

"Dried beans and squash!"

"And bundles of sticks to keep our fires burning."

There was a feast in Nicodemus that night.

Before we ate, Daddy said to us, "Johnny, Willie, Little Brother, I want you to remember this day. When someone says bad things about Indians, tell them the Osage Indians saved our lives in Nicodemus."

Keep the Lights Burning, Abbie

PETER and CONNIE ROOP

Abbie looked out the lighthouse window. Waves washed up on the rocks below. Out at sea, a ship sailed safely by.

"Will you sail to town today, Papa?" Abbie asked.

"Yes," Captain Burgess answered. "We need supplies, and Mama needs medicine. The weather is good now, so it's safe to go out in *Puffin*."

"But what if you don't get back today?" asked Abbie. "Who will take care of the lights?"

Papa smiled. "You will, Abbie."

"Oh no, Papa!" said Abbie. "I have never done it alone."

"You have trimmed the wicks before," said Papa. "You have cleaned the lamps and put in the oil. Mama is too sick to do it. Your sisters are too little. You must keep the lights burning, Abbie. Many ships count on our lighthouses."

Abbie followed Papa down the steps and to the shore. Their little boat, *Puffin*, pulled on its rope. Captain Burgess jumped into the boat and raised the sail.

"Keep the lights burning, Abbie!" he called.

"I will, Papa," Abbie cried. But the wind carried off her words. Abbie watched *Puffin* slide out to sea. She knew Papa was a fine sailor. He could sail in rain and fog. But if the wind blew up again, he could not sail back to Matinicus Rock today. The waves would be too high for the little boat. Then she would have to care for the lights.

Abbie looked up. The two lighthouse towers seemed as high as the sky.

That afternoon, Abbie helped Mahala write her letters. Esther helped Lydia cook supper. Everyone helped take care of Mama.

Outside, the sky turned gray. The wind put whitecaps on the waves. Another winter storm was coming. When the sun went down, Abbie put on her coat. She had to light the lamps.

Abbie ran up the lighthouse steps and stopped at the top to look out. The waves were so big that she could not even see Matinicus Island. She knew Papa could not sail back. Abbie was afraid. What if she could not light the lamps?

She picked up a box of matches. Her hands were shaking, but she struck a match. One by one, she lit all the lamps. Then she went to the other lighthouse tower and lit those lamps as well. Out at sea, a ship saw the lights. It steered away from the dangerous rocks.

That night, the wind blew hard. Abbie could not sleep. She kept thinking about the lights. What if they went out? A ship might crash.

Finally, Abbie got out of bed, put on her coat, and climbed the lighthouse steps. It was a good thing she had come. There was ice on the windows, so the lights could not be seen. All night long, Abbie climbed up and down, scraping ice off the windows. She checked each light. Not one went out.

In the morning, the wind still blew. Abbie blew out each light, trimmed each wick, and cleaned each lamp. She put in more oil. Then she went to breakfast. At last, she went to bed.

For more than a week, the wind and rain roared. For a while, the family had to move from their house into one of the strong towers. One morning, water ran under the tower door.

"My chickens!" Abbie cried. "They will be washed away."

Abbie ran out into the rain and waded to the henhouse. She put Patience under one arm. She pushed Hope and Charity into a basket. Just then she heard another big wave coming. It sounded like a train!

Abbie raced to the tower. "Let me in!" she yelled. Lydia opened the door. As Abbie ran inside, the wave

crashed over Matinicus Rock. It washed away the henhouse.
The girls pushed the tower door shut just before the wave
hit it. Abbie felt the lighthouse shake. She was shaking, too.
They had shut the door just in time.

Day after day, it snowed or rained. Abbie wished it
would stop. She was tired of the wind. She was tired of the
waves. She was tired of climbing the lighthouse steps. Most
of all, she was tired of eggs. The only thing left to eat was
eggs, and Abbie was sick of them.

Then one morning the waves seemed smaller, and the
wind did not blow so hard. Late that afternoon, the girls
heard a voice outside.

It was Papa. They ran to help him carry in the boxes.
There was medicine for Mama. There was oil for the lamps.
There was mail, and food and corn for Abbie's chickens.

"I was afraid for you," said Papa. "Every night I
watched for the lights. Every night I saw them. Then I knew
you were all right."

Abbie smiled. "I kept the lights burning, Papa."

Unit Four
Stories and People

The Story of Grandpa's Sled and the Pig

LAURA INGALLS WILDER

[**PART 1**]

When your Grandpa was a
boy, Laura, Sunday did not begin
on Sunday morning, as it does now.
It began at sundown on Saturday
night. Then everyone stopped every
kind of work or play.

Supper was solemn. After supper,
Grandpa's father read aloud a chapter
of the Bible, while everyone sat straight and
still in his chair. Then they all knelt down, and their father
said a long prayer. When he said, "Amen," they got up
from their knees and each took a candle and went to bed.
They must go straight to bed, with no playing, laughing, or
even talking.

Sunday morning they ate a cold breakfast, because nothing could be cooked on Sunday. Then they all dressed in their best clothes and walked to church. They walked, because hitching up the horses was work, and no work could be done on Sunday.

They must walk slowly and solemnly, looking straight ahead. They must not joke or laugh, or even smile. Grandpa and his two brothers walked ahead, and their father and mother walked behind them.

In church, Grandpa and his brothers must sit perfectly still for two long hours and listen to the sermon. They dared not fidget on the hard bench. They dared not swing their feet. They dared not turn their heads to look at the windows or the walls or the ceiling of the church. They must sit perfectly motionless, and never for one instant take their eyes from the preacher.

When church was over, they walked slowly home. They might talk on the way, but they must not talk loudly and they must never laugh or smile. At home they ate a cold dinner which had been cooked the day before. Then all the long afternoon they must sit in a row on a bench and study their catechism, until at last the sun went down and Sunday was over.

Now Grandpa's home was about halfway down the side of a steep hill. The road went from the top of the hill to the bottom, right past the front door, and in winter it was the best place for sliding downhill that you can possibly imagine.

One week Grandpa and his two brothers, James and George, were making a new sled. They worked at it every minute of their playtime. It was the best sled they had ever made, and it was so long that all three of them could sit on it, one behind the other. They planned to finish it in time to slide downhill Saturday afternoon. For every Saturday afternoon they had two or three hours to play.

But that week their father was cutting down trees in the Big Woods. He was working hard and he kept the boys working with him. They did all the morning chores by lantern light and were hard at work in the wood when the sun came up. They worked till dark, and then there were the chores to do, and after supper they had to go to bed so they could get up early in the morning.

They had no time to work on the sled until Saturday afternoon. Then they worked at it just as fast as they could, but they didn't get it finished till just as the sun went down Saturday night.

After the sun went down, they could not slide downhill, not even once. That would be breaking the Sabbath. So they put the sled in the shed behind the house, to wait until Sunday was over.

[PART 2]

All the two long hours in church next day, while they kept their feet still and their eyes on the preacher, they were thinking about the sled. At home while they ate dinner they couldn't think of anything else. After dinner their father sat down to read the Bible, and Grandpa and James and George sat as still as mice on their bench with their catechism. But they were thinking about the sled.

The sun shone brightly and the snow was smooth and glittering on the road; they could see it through the window. It was a perfect day for sliding downhill. They looked at their catechism and they thought about the new sled, and it seemed that Sunday would never end.

After a long time they heard a snore. They looked at their father, and they saw that his head had fallen against the back of his chair and he was fast asleep.

Then James looked at George, and James got up from the bench and tiptoed out of the room through the back door. George looked at Grandpa, and George tiptoed after James. And Grandpa looked fearfully at their father, but on tiptoe he followed George and left their father snoring.

They took their new sled and went quietly up to the top of the hill. They meant to slide down, just once. Then they would put the sled away, and slip back to their bench and the catechism before their father woke up.

James sat in front on the sled, then George, and then Grandpa, because he was the littlest. The sled started, at first slowly, then faster and faster. It was running, flying, down the long steep hill, but the boys dared not shout. They must slide silently past the house without waking their father.

There was no sound except the little whirr of the runners on the snow, and the wind rushing past.

Then just as the sled was swooping toward the house, a big black pig stepped out of the woods. He walked into the middle of the road and stood there.

The sled was going so fast it couldn't be stopped. There wasn't time to turn it. The sled went right under the hog and picked him up. With a squeal he sat down on James, and kept on squealing, long and loud and shrill, "Squee-ee-ee-ee! Squee-ee-ee-ee-ee-ee!"

They flashed by the house, the pig sitting in front, then James, then George, then Grandpa, and they saw their father standing in the doorway looking at them. They couldn't stop, they couldn't hide, there was no time to say

anything. Down the hill they went, the hog sitting on James and squealing all the way.

At the bottom of the hill they stopped. The hog jumped off James and ran away into the woods, still squealing.

The boys walked slowly and solemnly up the hill. They put the sled away. They sneaked into the house and slipped quietly to their places on the bench. Their father was reading his Bible. He looked up at them without saying a word.

Then he went on reading, and they studied their catechism.

But when the sun went down and the Sabbath day was over, their father took them out to the woodshed and tanned their jackets, first James, then George, then Grandpa.

116

Winter Walk

AILEEN FISHER

I like days in winter
when paths are packed with snow
and feet make creaky footsteps
wherever footsteps go,

       and

I like days in winter
when snow lies soft and deep
and footsteps go so quietly
you'd think they were asleep.

Harriet Tubman

HELEN WEBBER

In the mid-1800s people were thinking about building a railroad from east to west across our country. Another kind of railroad was already running from south to north. This was called the Underground Railroad.

The Underground Railroad was not really under the ground, and it was not really a railroad. It was a secret group of people who helped black slaves escape to freedom in the North. The home of each member of the group was a "station" on the "railroad." Some members acted as "conductors" to lead the slaves to safety. One of the bravest of these conductors was Harriet Tubman.

118

Harriet was born a slave in Maryland in about 1820. She lived with her parents and ten brothers and sisters in a one-room cabin with a dirt floor and no windows. When she was only five years old, her owner sent her out to work as a servant. But Harriet did not make a good servant. Her restless desire to be free made her masters angry, and she was often whipped and treated cruelly.

Later Harriet worked outdoors, where she was happier. Although she was tiny, she worked as well as a grown man in the fields and in the woods. Still, she was known as a troublemaker. All the while her hatred of slavery grew.

When she was a teenager, Harriet was hit on the head with a heavy weight while trying to save another slave from being punished. She was unconscious for several days and suffered from this wound for the rest of her life.

In 1849 Harriet decided to run away. With the help of a white friend who was a member of the Underground Railroad, she started north. She traveled mostly alone and mostly by night. She knew that to keep from getting lost she must follow the North Star. This is the bright star next to the group of stars that Harriet called the Drinking Gourd. Now most people call it the Big Dipper or the Great Bear.

When Harriet reached the North, where slavery was against the law, she settled down to work and to enjoy her new freedom. Soon, however, she risked that freedom to go back to the South and help her sister escape. Then Harriet knew that this was the work she wanted to do. After that she went south many more times and guided more than three hundred slaves to freedom.

She was called "Moses" because she led her people to a Promised Land. Sometimes she went south dressed as a man and sometimes as a very old woman. Slave owners knew that Moses was stealing slaves out from under their noses, but they could never catch her.

Many other people were fighting slavery at that time along with Harriet. The most famous of these fighters was old John Brown. The old man planned to make war against the slave owners. Harriet helped him get men to join his army. John Brown's plan failed. Then the Civil War broke out—the war that would end slavery in America forever.

During the Civil War, Harriet worked in South Carolina for the Union Army, first as a nurse and later as a scout. She explored the countryside at night to find out what was happening. The information she gathered helped free hundreds more slaves.

After the war was over and all the slaves were free, Harriet went back north and went on helping her people. She opened a home for the poor and sick among them. Nothing in her long and useful life, however, gave her more happiness than her work with the Underground Railroad. She often used to say, "On my Underground Railroad I never ran my train off the track. And I never lost a passenger."

Follow the Drinking Gourd

AN AMERICAN FOLK SONG

When the sun comes back and the first quail calls,
Follow the drinking gourd;
For the old man is waiting for to carry you to freedom
If you follow the drinking gourd.

The river bank will make a very good road,
The dead trees show you the way;
Left foot, peg foot, traveling on,
Follow the drinking gourd.

Martin and Abraham Lincoln

CATHERINE CATE COBLENTZ

It was a hot summer day in Washington, D.C., during the Civil War. As usual, Martin Emery was wearing his little Union Army uniform. He had been helping his neighbor, Snowden, sell vegetables in the streets. They had worked hard all morning. Now Martin looked pale and tired, so Snowden left him to rest near the U.S. Capitol.

[PART 1]

The sun was hot. Martin went over and sat down on the stone steps of the Capitol. The steps were clean and cool. His eyes closed a little as he leaned back, his head resting against the stone at one side.

Then, as always when he was alone and it was still, Martin began thinking about his father. A lump began to grow in his throat.

He heard someone coming down the steps behind him. There was plenty of room, so Martin didn't move. He just sat there and watched dreamily as a long shadow moved over the step he was on. The shadow went slither-sliding

down the step ahead. And the next. And the next. And the next.

Then the shadow stopped and stayed in one place. A voice just behind Martin said, "Well, well! How's my little soldier?"

Soldier! When his father's friends had said that, Martin had always done as his father had taught him, jumped to his feet and saluted. So, forgetting how tired and sad he was, he sprang to his feet, flinging his head back and his hand up at the same time.

As his fingers touched the visor of his blue cap, Martin's heart began to thud like a drum. There stood Abraham Lincoln looking down at him. His sad face was losing its look of worry and breaking slowly into a smile. Abraham Lincoln, himself!

"What is your name, soldier?" the great man asked, gravely returning the salute.

Martin told him.

"Where were you born, Martin?"

"In Vermont. In a log cabin."

The man nodded. "I was born in a log cabin, too."

"I know. Mother told me. She said some day I might get to be President like you."

"All mothers say that, Martin. What does your father say?"

"I don't know." Martin's voice slowed. "You see, he is away. He used to be a cobbler, but now he is your soldier."

"What regiment? And where is he now?"

The lump in Martin's throat was growing larger. It was difficult to make words come. "The First Vermont—" he managed to say, and then the sobs had him. "He's in Andersonville Prison."

The great man was bending over. Strong arms were lifting Martin. In another moment the man had taken Martin's place on the steps. Martin was folded into his lap.

The boy's face was hidden now in Abraham Lincoln's vest.

Abraham Lincoln just sat there, holding the little boy whose sobbing had been kept back for so long. A great hand patted him gently between the shoulders. When Martin grew quieter, the man began to talk.

"So your father is a cobbler. Is he a good cobbler, Martin?"

Martin nodded his head so hard that his nose went up and down against Abraham Lincoln's ribs.

"Good cobblers are mighty important," said the man. "Never made a pair of shoes myself. But I saw a boy once that needed some mighty bad." The President settled his back a little more comfortably into the corner of the step and the wall.

"It happened when I was postmaster back in Illinois. People didn't write many letters in those days, so I carried them in my hat. One cold day as I was going along with the letters in my hat, I saw Ab Trout. He was as barefoot as the day he was born and was chopping a pile of logs from an old barn that had been torn down. The logs were gnarled and tough. Ab's ax kept going slower and slower.

"'What do you get for this job, Ab?' I asked him.

"'A dollar.'

"'What do you aim to do with it?'

"'Buy a pair of shoes,' he said.

"'You'll never get one shoe at this rate, Ab,' I told him. 'Better go in and warm yourself, and you'll work faster.' So he did. Funniest thing, Martin. When Ab came out, that wood was all chopped! Now what do you think of that?"

Martin sat up and looked straight at Abraham Lincoln. "I think you chopped that wood," he said.

"Maybe you're right." Lincoln smiled. "After all, folks must help each other."

Martin nodded. "I help my mother all I can," he said. "I fix the rough places in my sisters' shoes. I can do it almost as well as Father did. Mother says it helps a lot."

"I am sure it does." The President nodded.

"Vermont is a long way off," he went on. "Tell me, how do you happen to be here, Martin?"

Martin wiped the last tear from his cheek with the handkerchief Mr. Lincoln handed him. He could talk now. He wanted to.

[PART 2]

"Father went to war," Martin began. "He was stationed at a fort near Alexandria. After a time he found a house near the fort, and he sent for Mother and me and my sisters. We came on the train. At first we saw Father often.

Then one night when some of the soldiers were sent out to take a railroad bridge, Father was captured. He was sent to prison."

"How does your mother manage to take care of you?" asked Abraham Lincoln.

"Well, it's like you said. Folks help. The soldiers—Father's friends—bring their mending to her. They ask her to cook for them. Sometimes they bring their washing for her to do. They pay as much as they can. The soldiers give us cloth for our clothes, too.

"And Snowden helps. Snowden is my friend. He sells vegetables from his cart and I help him. Snowden fills the basket under the seat with vegetables and calls them leftovers. He gives the basket to Mother. But the vegetables aren't leftovers. Not really."

Martin didn't tell about his mother's prayer for flour and sugar and butter and eggs. He didn't need to. Abraham Lincoln seemed to know all about that prayer.

"Hmm!" he began. "It seems to me, Martin, that part of this job of helping belongs to the army—your father's army and mine. I will speak to somebody, and I'm pretty sure there will be food from the army stores every week for your mother. Things that Snowden and the soldiers can't supply, like butter and bacon and other things."

There wasn't any lump in Martin's throat now. He felt wonderful. But for some reason the tears began to pour down his face.

The man pretended not to see. Instead, he raised himself to his feet, and a sudden frown grew deep between his eyes. "It's my shoe, Martin," he explained. "There's a nail sticking right into my foot. I keep forgetting to have it fixed."

"Oh, wait," cried Martin. "I can help you." He darted off to a pile of stones by the steps. Luckily he found the kind he wanted right away. When he came back Abraham Lincoln was sitting on the steps with his shoe off, waiting to be helped.

Martin sat down beside him. He slipped one stone inside the great shoe. With the other he pounded hard on the sole.

"My father showed me how," he boasted between pounds. "He is a good cobbler."

Abraham Lincoln smiled. "I'd like to be a cobbler myself, Martin. A good cobbler."

"That's what I am going to be," said Martin.

Down the street he could see Snowden's cart moving nearer. He could hear the sound of Nellie's bell and the

jingle of her harness. He finished the shoe and gave it to Abraham Lincoln.

The man put on the shoe. He stood up and set his foot down carefully where the nail had been. He pressed harder, while Martin watched his face. There was no frown between Abraham Lincoln's eyes.

"It's a good job, Martin," he said. "It feels just fine." He paused and looked over Martin's head, far into the distance. The worry had gone now from the President's face. "You have helped me, Martin," he said, "more than you know!"

Martin said nothing. He only slipped his hand inside Abraham Lincoln's. They came down the steps together.

They were waiting when Snowden and Nellie arrived.

Snowden's mouth popped wide open. Nellie stopped. She flicked her ears, and Snowden swept off his hat.

The man beside Martin lifted his hat gravely in return. Then he bent and raised Martin high in the air and put him on the seat beside Snowden.

"Good-bye, soldier," he said.

Martin saluted. Snowden saluted. Abraham Lincoln saluted. Nellie started toward home.

An American Painter

ELIZABETH WASHBURN

Mary Cassatt is one of America's most famous artists. Her paintings can be seen in museums here and around the world. Mary lived from 1844 to 1926. She did her work at a time when few women were educated or had careers.

Breakfast in Bed,   1897

When Mary was a young girl, the Cassatts lived in Paris, France, for a few years. Here Mary had a chance to see many art exhibits. She liked to study the work of the French artists and longed to be an artist herself. By the time she was sixteen years old, Mary had decided to make art her life's work.

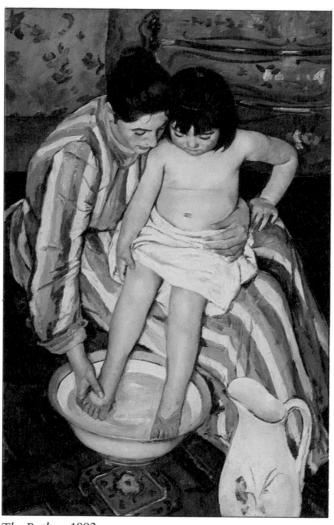

The Bath, 1892

The Boating Party, 1893-94

Even though Mary's father did not like the idea, he finally agreed that she could study art. In 1861 she became a student at the Pennsylvania Academy of Fine Arts. The work there soon became boring. There were no live models in women's classes. Instead, the students drew sketches of the same statues over and over and made copies of paintings. Mary didn't mind copying paintings, but the really great ones were in Europe.

It took five more years, but at last Mary's father agreed that she could study in Europe. She spent some time in Italy and Spain but settled in Paris. Paris was the center for young artists and for all that was new in painting.

Mary's dreams came true. She studied long and hard and became a fine artist. Her paintings are full of life and color and warmth. Although Mary never married, she was very fond of children. She usually painted pictures of women, of children, or of babies in their mother's arms. The pictures on these pages are examples of the feeling Mary Cassatt put into her work.

Mother and Child, 1889

Paul Bunyan

BARBARA EMBERLEY

When this country was young, most of it was one great forest stretching from the Atlantic to the Pacific. At that time, there lived mighty men who were twice as big and twice as strong as any men who have lived before or since. It was their job to cut down huge trees, chop them into logs, and send them down the river to be cut up into lumber. These men were called loggers or lumberjacks.

As I said, the loggers were mighty men. The mightiest, the biggest, and the strongest of them all was Paul Bunyan. He was so big that he used to comb his long beard with an old pine tree he yanked right out of the ground.

Paul was strong. You won't forget it when I tell you that he could squeeze water out of a boulder. He could drive stumps into the ground with his bare fists. It's a good thing that he was kind and gentle and would only pick on someone his own size.

Paul used most of his strength for logging—like the time he dug himself a river to help move his logs.

He was cutting trees one morning up in Minnesota. He had to get them to the sawmill, which was in New Orleans, and he decided the best way to do it would be by river—but there was no river.

So Paul had a light lunch of 19 pounds of sausage, 6 hams, 8 loaves of bread, and 231 flapjacks. Each flapjack was slathered with a pound of butter and a quart of maple syrup. It was a skimpy lunch for Paul, but he figured on eating a hearty supper to make up for it. Paul dug his river that afternoon, and he called it the Mississippi. As far as I know, that is what it is called to this day.

When Paul was a boy, he got hold of all the books that had ever been written. He took them up to a cave in Canada and read them. He had just finished the last book when a snowflake blew into his cave. The snowflake was the most brilliant blue he had ever seen.

It snowed and snowed and snowed, covering everything with a blanket of blue. When it stopped snowing, Paul decided to take a walk. He was down by Niagara Falls when he noticed a big, blue oxtail sticking out of the snow. And what should he find on the other end of the big blue oxtail but a big blue ox! The snow had turned that ox blue from head to toe.

Paul carried the ox back to his cave to warm him up and to give him some food. He called his ox *Bébé*, which is

138

French-Canadian for *Baby*. "Babe" grew to be so big that
he measured forty-two ax handles from horn to horn, and
he grew so heavy that he left hoof marks in solid rock. Babe
and Paul became great friends.

Now that Paul had a great blue ox to help him, it was
natural that he should decide to go logging. It was also
natural that he had some of the biggest men who walked
the woods working for him. Even the chore boy was twelve
feet tall. Everyone picked on him because he was too little to
fight back.

Paul's crew slept in a bunkhouse that was so tall it had
a hinged chimney to let the sun go by. There was a chow
hall so long that the waiters had to ride on horseback to get
around. The flapjack griddle was so big that it took three

139

sharp-eyed men four days to look across it. It took six men three days skating around it, with hog fat strapped to their shoes, to get it greased.

Paul and his men put the camp buildings on runners, hitched them up to Babe, and they all went back and forth across this great country, clearing the land. They cleared the West so the cattle could graze. They cleared Kansas for wheat and Iowa for corn—just to mention a few of the states they worked in.

When Paul and Babe had finished their work, they went deep into the woods to take a good, long rest. And as far as anyone knows, they are resting still.

Watch the Stars Come Out

RIKI LEVINSON

Grandma told me that when her mama was a little girl she had red hair—just like me.

Grandma's mama loved to go to bed early and watch the stars come out—just like me.

Every Friday night, after the dishes were put away, Grandma's mama would come to her room and tell her this special story.

When I was a little girl, my big brother and I went on a big boat to America. Mama and Papa and Sister were waiting there for us.

My aunt, Mama's sister, took us to the boat. She didn't bring my two little brothers. They were too small. They would come on a boat when they were older.

Aunt gave us a barrel full of dried fruit. She asked an old lady to watch over us. And she did. She also ate our dried fruit.

The old lady and Brother and I went down the steps to our room. I counted the steps as we carried our bundles down, but there were so many that I forgot to count after a while.

Sometimes the boat rocked back and forth—it was fun! Some people didn't like it—they got sick. The old lady got very, very sick. She died.

Brother told me not to worry. He would take care of me—he was ten.

At night when I went to sleep, I couldn't see the stars come out in the sky. That made me sad.

Each morning when we got up, Brother put a mark on his stick. I counted them—twenty-three.

The last morning we looked across the water. There were two islands near each other. One of them had a statue standing on it—a lady with a crown. Everyone got very excited and waved to her. I did too.

At noon the boat stopped. We carried our bundles down the plank.

I started to cry. I did not see Mama and Papa and Sister.

A sailor told me not to worry—we would see them soon. First we had to go on another boat to a place on an island.

144

We carried our bundles into a big, big room. Brother and I went into a small room with all the other children without mamas and papas.

A lady looked at me all over. I wondered why.

I waited for Brother. The lady looked at him too.

The next day we went on a ferry. The land came closer and closer as we watched. Everyone waved. We did too.

Mama and Papa and Sister were there!

We went on a trolley to our home. Mama said it was a palace.

Mama's palace was on the top floor. I counted the steps as we walked up—fifty-two!

Mama and Papa's room was in the middle. Our room was in the front. And in the back was the kitchen with a big black stove.

Mama warmed a big pot of water on the stove. She poured some into the sink and helped me climb in to wash.

Mama washed my hair, and when it was dry, she brushed it. It felt good.

Sister gave us cookies and glasses of tea.

I was very tired.

I kissed Mama and Sister good-night. Papa patted me on my head and said I was his little princess.

I went into our room and climbed into Sister's bed. It was right next to the window.

I watched the stars come out. One, two, three.

This Friday night I will go to bed very early and watch the stars come out in the sky. I hope Grandma will come to my room and tell me another special story.

Doña Felisa

FRANCO COUR

On Wednesday mornings the city hall in San Juan, Puerto Rico, became the house of the people. Every week on that day, the mayor of San Juan, Felisa Rincón de Gautier, held open house. Wearing one of the astonishing hats that were her trademark, she came into the council room where hundreds of people waited. She wished a good day to these people, *"Buenos días, amigos."* They answered, *"Buenos días, Doña Felisa."*

Then Doña Felisa took her seat at a simple table. One by one the people came up for a few moments of quiet talk. She helped them to get whatever it was they needed—school shoes, medical care, or a place to live. Perhaps just comfort and advice were needed. She would not leave the room until she had talked with everyone there.

The story of how Doña Felisa became mayor of the capital city of Puerto Rico is partly a story of changing ideas about the place of women in public life.

Felisa was the eldest of eight children in a well-to-do family. When she was twelve years old, her mother died. After a time, her father decided that he needed his eldest daughter to run the household. Felisa, who had hoped to become a doctor, had to leave high school. It would have been very hard for a young girl, brought up in the old Spanish way, to argue with her father.

Felisa went on being an obedient daughter. Her father decided that he would move his family to the country and spend only weekends with them. Although she missed the city, Felisa had to go to the country to take care of her younger brothers and sisters and to run the family farm. She became an able manager.

At last a time came when Felisa would no longer bow to every wish of her father. In 1917 Congress had passed a law making Puerto Ricans citizens of the United States. In 1920 it had passed another law giving women on the mainland the right to vote. After some years Puerto Rico also gave women that right. Felisa wanted to register to vote, but her father objected. This time, however, she would not give in. She won her father's consent and was proud to be among the first women to sign the voting register.

When she registered to vote, she joined the political party of Luis Muñoz Marín. From that day on, Felisa made herself useful to her political party. Her special job was to bring the party's promise of reform to the poor people of San Juan. She made friends with these people.

After years of work, Doña Felisa was well known and loved in San Juan. She was easily elected mayor in 1946 and many other times. She was the mayor of San Juan for twenty-two years, until 1968.

During that time Doña Felisa cleaned up the city. She built a chain of nursery schools and improved the hospitals. She made sure that the poor children of the city had shoes and clothes and toys at Christmas. And she encouraged Puerto Rican women to be active in public life. But perhaps she is best remembered for her Wednesdays—those days when she held open house and the city hall became the house of the people.

Rufus M.

ELEANOR ESTES

Rufus Moffat is too young to go to school. He has not yet learned how to read or how to write his name. One day he sees his older brother and sisters reading library books. He decides that he wants a book from the library too, but Rufus does not have a library card. The librarian tells him he must fill out an application in order to get a card.

The lady put a piece of paper covered with a lot of printing in front of Rufus, dipped a pen in the ink well and gave it to him.

"All right," she said. "Here's your application. Write your name here."

All the writing Rufus had ever done before had been on big pieces of brown wrapping paper with lots of room on them. Rufus had often covered those great sheets of paper with his own kind of writing at home. Lines up and down.

But on this paper there wasn't much space. It was already covered with writing. However, there was a tiny, little empty space, and that was where Rufus must write his name, the lady said. So, little space or not, Rufus confidently grasped the pen with his left hand and dug it into the paper. He was not accustomed to pens, having always worked with pencils until now, and he made a great many holes and blots and scratches.

"Gracious," said the lady. "Don't bear down so hard! And why don't you hold it in your right hand?" she asked, moving the pen back into his right hand.

Rufus started again scraping his lines up and down and all over the page, this time using his right hand. Wherever there was an empty space he wrote. He even wrote over some of the print for good measure. Then he waited for the lady, who had gone off to get a book for some man, to come back and look.

"Oh," she said as she settled herself in her swivel chair, "is that the way you write? Well . . . it's nice, but what does it say?"

"Says Rufus Moffat. My name."

Apparently these lines up and down did not spell Rufus Moffat to this lady. She shook her head.

"It's nice," she repeated. "Very nice. But nobody but you knows what it says. You have to learn to write your name better than that before you can join the library."

Rufus was silent. He had come to the library all by himself, gone back home to wash his hands, and come back because he wanted to take books home and read them the way the others did. He had worked hard. He did not like to think he might have to go home without a book.

The library lady looked at him a moment and then she said quickly before he could get himself all the way off the big chair, "Maybe you can *print* your name."

Rufus looked at her hopefully. He thought he could write better than he could print, for his writing certainly looked to him exactly like all grown people's writing. Still he'd try to print if that was what she wanted.

The lady printed some letters on the top of a piece of paper. "There," she said. "That's your name. Copy it ten times and then we'll try it on another application."

Rufus worked hard. He worked so hard the knuckles showed white on his brown fist. He worked for a long, long time, now with his right hand and now with his left. Sometimes a boy or a girl came in, looked over his shoulder and watched, but he paid no attention. From time to time the lady studied his work, and she said, "That's fine. That's fine." At last she said, "Well, maybe now we can try." And she gave him another application.

All Rufus could get, with his large, generous letters, in that tiny, little space where he was supposed to print his name, was R-U-F. The other letters he scattered here and there on the card. The lady did not like this either. She gave him still another blank. Rufus tried to print smaller and this time he got RUFUS in the space, and also he crowded an M at the end. Since he was doing so well now, the lady herself printed the *offat* part of Moffat on the next line.

"This will have to do," she said. "Now take this home

and ask your mother to sign it on the other side. Bring it back on Thursday and you'll get your card."

Rufus's face was shiny and streaked with dirt where he had rubbed it. He never knew there was all this work to getting a book. The other Moffats just came in and got books. Well, maybe they had had to do this once too.

Rufus held his hard-earned application in one hand and steered his scooter with the other. When he reached home Joey, Jane and Sylvie were not around any longer. Mama signed his card for him, saying, "My! So you've learned how to write!"

"Print," corrected Rufus.

Mama kissed Rufus and he went back out. The lady had said to come back on Thursday, but he wanted a book today. When the other Moffats came home, he'd be sitting on the top step of the porch, reading. That would surprise them.

Unit Five
Our Country Today

Maria Martinez:
Pueblo Potter

STEVE OSBORN

The story of Maria Martinez began a thousand years before she was born. At that time the Anasazi Indians lived in the area that is now called New Mexico. Their way of life was good, and they did many things well. They lived in large cities filled with tall, stone houses. They built straight roads and grew wide fields of corn. They also made beautiful clay pots. They used these pots for cooking and for storing food and water. On the outside of the pots, they painted wonderful pictures and designs. They painted the finest pots with a shiny black color that gleamed in the sunlight.

The Anasazis ruled over the land that is now New Mexico for hundreds of years. Then, about four hundred years ago, white people came and fought a war against them. The Anasazis lost the war, and the white people became the new rulers of the land.

The Anasazis could no longer build their own cities or make their own roads. The white people even gave them a new name—Pueblo Indians—instead of Anasazis.

In the year 1881 a Pueblo Indian girl was born in a small village in New Mexico. Her real name was Poveka, but the white people called her Maria. Maria's village was very poor. Not many people had jobs.

When Maria was born, only a few Pueblos were still making pots. Their pots were good, but they were not nearly so beautiful as the old Anasazi pots. The Pueblos had forgotten how to make pots in the old way.

Maria loved pots and started making them when she was still a little girl. She learned quickly. Soon she was the best potter in the village. The other Pueblos were amazed at how smooth and round her pots were. But Maria was not satisfied. She had seen some of the old Anasazi pots, and she

wanted to learn how they were made. Every day, Maria studied the old pots and tried to make new ones in the same way.

When Maria was twenty-three years old, she married Julian Martinez. Julian was also interested in the old pots. He did not know how to make them, but he did know how to paint beautiful pictures and designs. So Maria and Julian began working together. When Maria finished shaping a pot, Julian would paint it. Their pots were wonderful. They still had not discovered how to make pots in the old way, but they were getting close.

One day a man found some pieces of an old Anasazi pot. The pieces were a shiny black color that he had never seen before. He took the pieces to Maria and Julian. He asked whether they knew how to make a pot of the same color. For a whole year Maria and Julian tried. Then one day they succeeded. They made a shiny black pot that was just like the old Anasazi pots.

The man came back and bought the pot. He asked
Maria and Julian to make more. Soon Maria and Julian
were making and selling many of the beautiful, black pots.
As time went by, they kept improving their pots. They
discovered how to make them shinier. They also figured out
a new method for drawing designs on the pots. In some
ways their pots were even more beautiful than the old
Anasazi pots.

Maria and Julian earned a lot of money from their
pots. Instead of keeping the money for themselves, they
shared it with the other Pueblos. They also shared what they
had learned by teaching many Pueblos to make pots in the
old way.

Things began to change for the Pueblos. Once again
they were making beautiful clay pots. Their pots were some
of the best in the world. Maria's were still the most famous,
but those of other Pueblo potters became well known too.
People from all over the world bought the pots and asked
for more.

Both Maria and Julian are dead now, but the Pueblos
will never forget them. Thanks to Maria and Julian, the art
that began more than a thousand years ago will last for a
long time to come.

The Apollo Program

SEYMOUR SIMON

[PART 1]

From earliest times, people gazed up at the moon and wondered about it. Was the moon a world like ours? Were there living things on the moon? Would we ever be able to travel to the moon?

Over the years, scientists learned much about the moon by studying it from Earth with telescopes and other instruments. But many things were still unknown. Then in 1961, the United States government decided to try to send a person to the moon within the next ten years. This space program was named Apollo.

Before the space age, no one had ever seen the far side of the moon. That's because the same side of the moon always faces Earth. Then in 1968, a spaceship from Earth went around the moon. Astronauts in the Apollo 8 spaceship flew over the far side of the moon.

Photographs of the moon's far side were taken from Apollo spaceships. The far side has craters and mountains,

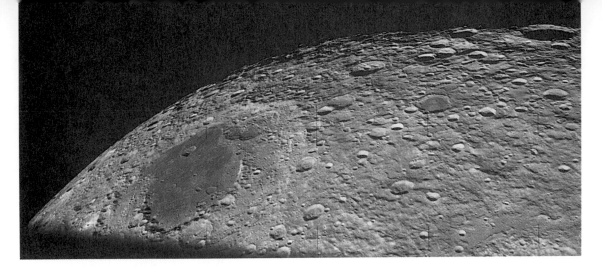

much like those on the side of the moon we see from Earth.
Unlike the side we see, however, the far side has few flat
lands, or "seas."

On July 20, 1969, Neil Armstrong became the first
person to set foot on the moon. Armstrong was one of the
astronauts on the Apollo 11 space flight. He was shortly
followed by Edwin Aldrin, another member of the Apollo
11 crew.

Neil Armstrong's footprints
on the moon marked the first
time that human beings walked
on ground that was not on
Earth. The footprints may last
for a million years or longer.
That is because there is no air
on the moon and no winds to
blow the dust around.

The astronauts could jump much higher on the moon than on Earth. People weigh much less on the moon than they do on Earth. The moon's gravity is one-sixth that of Earth's. Gravity causes objects to have weight. In places where there is less gravity, you weigh less and you can jump higher. That's why the astronauts could leap about on the moon's surface. To find out what you would weigh on the moon, divide your weight by six.

The astronauts discovered that the moon is a silent, strange place. The moon has no air. Air carries sound. With no air, the moon is completely silent. Even when the astronauts broke rocks or used the rockets on their spaceship, sound could not be heard.

The sky on the moon is always black. Stars shine all the time. On Earth, we can see the stars only at night.

[PART 2]

The moon does not have air, water, clouds, rain, or snow. It does not have weather. But the surface of the moon does warm up and cool off. The ground gets very hot or very cold because there is no air to spread the heat. The temperatures in the daytime can be above the boiling point of water. At night, the temperature can drop hundreds of degrees below zero. The astronauts' space suits kept their

164

bodies at the right temperature. The astronauts carried tanks on their backs which contained the air they needed for breathing.

Without air and water, the moon's surface has not worn away very much. The surface has changed so little that it holds clues to the early history of the moon. The astronauts searched for these clues. They collected rocks and brought them back to Earth for study by scientists. They drilled holes in the moon to look beneath the surface. They set up instruments to find moonquakes and to learn about other conditions on the moon. They photographed whatever they saw.

Each Apollo crew brought back more information about the moon. The astronauts of Apollo 15 stayed nearly sixty-seven hours on the moon. They returned with 173 pounds of moon rocks and soil. Scientists all over the world studied the information the astronauts brought back. They learned that the moon is about the same age as Earth. But

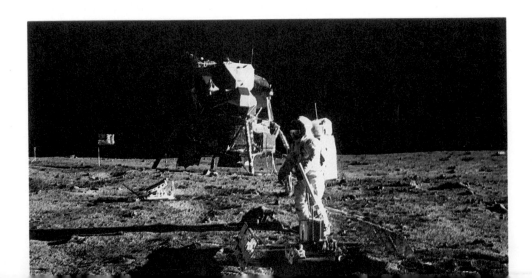

the moon's soil and rocks are different from Earth's. For instance, moon rocks contain no water at all, while almost all rocks on Earth contain a small amount of water.

Apollo 17 was the last spaceship to carry people to the moon. It was launched in December, 1972. The astronauts of Apollo 17 discovered the oldest rock ever found on the moon. Scientists on Earth tested the rock. They discovered that it was more than 4,500 million years old. They named it the Genesis rock. Before the astronauts returned to Earth, they left a plaque on the moon showing the history of moon travel. They also left a falcon feather and a four-leaf clover. The feather and the four-leaf clover stand for the living things of Earth.

Scientists learned much about the moon from the Apollo space flights. They found the answers to many questions they had. In science, however, the answer to one question often raises a new question. For example, the flights around the moon showed what the far side of the moon looks like. Now scientists wonder why the far side of the moon has fewer flat lands than the near side. Much about the moon still remains a mystery.

City Rain

RACHEL FIELD

Rain in the city!
  I love to see it fall
Slantwise where the buildings crowd
  Red brick and all.
Streets of shiny wetness
  Where the taxis go,
With people and umbrellas all
  Bobbing to and fro.

Rain in the city!
  I love to hear it drip
When I am cosy in my room
  Snug as any ship,
With toys spread on the table,
  With a picture book or two,
And the rain like a rumbling tune that sings
  Through everything I do.

Martin Luther King, Jr.

FRANCO COUR

Every American knows that black people were first brought to this country as slaves. It took a long civil war to set them free. As free Americans, black people should have had the rights to live, to work, and to go to school wherever they wished. In many places, however, they were not given these rights, which are called *civil rights*. In some states they were not even allowed to vote.

Martin Luther King, Jr., was one of the leaders in the fight for civil rights. He was a minister who became a hero to black people. All people who cared about freedom and peace admired him for his courage. King's fight for civil rights began in Montgomery, Alabama, in 1955.

At that time there were some unfair laws in Montgomery. One said that black people had to sit in the back of the bus. Another said that they had to give up their seats if white people were standing.

168

One winter day a black woman named Rosa Parks was riding a bus home. She was tired after a long day's work. The bus that she was on became crowded. The driver ordered Mrs. Parks to give her seat to a white man. With quiet courage, she refused. Then the police came and arrested her.

Black people were very angry to hear how Mrs. Parks had been treated. They knew that the law was wrong. Tired of being treated unfairly because they were black, they decided to *boycott* the buses. This meant that they would not ride them at all. If all the black people of Montgomery did not ride the buses, the bus company would lose a great deal of money.

King was the leader of this boycott. For a whole year thousands of blacks did not ride the buses. Instead, they went to their jobs any way they could. Many people walked for miles, and some even rode mules.

News of the boycott spread all over the country. Many Americans, both black and white, agreed with the blacks of

Montgomery. They did what they could to help change the laws. Of course, the bus company lost money. At last the fighters for civil rights won, and the unfair laws in Montgomery were changed.

King was proud that this change had been brought about without the use of violence. He thought that was the best way to fight for civil rights. People who did not like King sometimes used violence against him, however. His house was bombed, and once he was even stabbed. But he never allowed himself or his followers to use violence in return.

All across America, fighters for civil rights worked hard to change unfair laws. King led them in this fight. He was even willing to go to jail many times for breaking laws that he knew were unfair.

In August of 1963 King led his followers in a march on Washington, our country's capital. The marchers wanted to remind the government that blacks still did not have all of their civil rights. On that summer day King spoke about his dream for the future of our country:

I have a dream today that my four little children will one day live in a nation where they will not be judged by the color of their skin but by the content of their

character. I have a dream today. I have a dream that one day little black boys and black girls will be able to join hands with little white boys and white girls and walk together as sisters and brothers. All of God's children . . . will be able to join hands and sing in the words of the old Negro spiritual, "Free at last! Free at last! Thank God Almighty, we are free at last!"

For many years King worked hard to make his dream come true. Then, suddenly, his life ended. Some people still hated King because of the work he was doing. One of these people shot him to death in 1968. King was only thirty-nine years old.

King died, but his dream did not die with him. Many people have carried on the work that he began. These people have kept the dream of Martin Luther King alive.

Gloria Who Might Be My Best Friend

ANN CAMERON

If you have a girl for a friend, people find out and tease you. That's why I didn't want a girl for a friend—not until this summer, when I met Gloria.

It happened one afternoon when I was walking down the street by myself. My mother was visiting a friend of hers, and my brother, Huey, was visiting a friend of his. There aren't any kids my age in my neighborhood. I was walking down the street feeling lonely, wishing I had a friend to visit too.

172

A block from our house I saw a moving van in front of a brown house. Men were carrying in chairs and tables and bookcases and boxes full of I don't know what. I watched for a while, and then suddenly I heard a voice right behind me.

"Who are you?"

I turned around, and there was a girl in a yellow shirt. She looked about the same age as me. She had curly hair

that was braided into two pigtails with red ribbons at the ends.

"I'm Julian," I said. "Who are you?"

"I'm Gloria," she said. "I come from Newport. Do you know where Newport is?"

I wasn't sure, but I didn't tell Gloria. "It's a town on the ocean," I said.

"Right," Gloria said. "Can you turn a cartwheel?"

She turned sideways and did two cartwheels on the grass.

I had never tried a cartwheel before, but I tried to copy Gloria. My hands went down in the grass, my feet went up in the air, and—I fell over.

I looked at Gloria to see if she was laughing at me. If she was, I was going to go home and forget about her.

But she just looked at me very seriously and said, "It takes practice." Then I liked her.

"Would you like to come over to my house?" I said.

"All right," Gloria said, "if it's all right with my mother." She ran into the house and asked.

It was all right, so Gloria and I went to my house, and I showed her my room and my games and my rock collection. Then I made lemonade, and we sat at the kitchen table and drank it.

"I wish you'd live here a long time," I told Gloria.
Gloria said, "I wish I would too."

"I know the best way to make wishes," Gloria said.

"What's that?" I asked.

"First you make a kite. Do you know how to make one?"

"Yes," I said, "I know how."

We went out into the garage and spread out sticks and newspaper and made a kite. I fastened on the kite string, and then I went to the closet and got rags for the tail.

"Do you have some paper and two pencils?" Gloria asked. "Because now we make the wishes."

I didn't know what she was planning, but I went into the house and got pencils and paper.

"All right," Gloria said. "Every wish you want to have come true you write on a long, thin piece of paper. You don't tell me your wishes, and I don't tell you mine. If you tell, your wishes don't come true. Also, if you look at the other person's wishes, your wishes don't come true."

Gloria sat down on the garage floor and started writing her wishes. I went to the other side of the garage and wrote mine.

"How many wishes did you make?" Gloria asked.

"Five," I said. "How many did you make?"

"Two," Gloria said.

I wondered what they were.

"Now we put the wishes on the tail of the kite," Gloria said. "Every time we tie a piece of rag on the tail, we put one wish in the knot. You can put yours in first."

I tied my wishes onto the tail of the kite, and then Gloria tied hers on. Then we ran through the back yard with the kite and went into the open field beyond the yard.

The kite started to rise. The tail jerked heavily, like a long white snake. In a minute the kite passed the roof of my house and was climbing toward the sun.

We stood in the open field, looking up at it. "I know it's going to work!" Gloria said.

"How do you know?"

"When we take the kite down," Gloria told me, "there shouldn't be any wishes left in the tail. When the wind takes all your wishes, you know they'll come true."

The kite stayed up for a long time. We both held the string. The kite looked like a tiny black spot in the sun, and my neck got stiff from looking up at it.

"Shall we pull it in?" I asked.

"All right," Gloria said.

We drew the string in more and more until finally, like a tired bird, the kite fell at our feet.

We looked at the tail. All of our wishes were gone. Probably they were still flying higher and higher in the wind.

"Gloria," I said, "did you wish we would be friends?"

"You're not supposed to ask me that!" Gloria said.

"I'm sorry," I answered. But inside I was smiling. I had guessed one thing Gloria had wished for. I was pretty sure we would be friends.

two friends

NIKKI GIOVANNI

lydia and shirley have
two pierced ears and
two bare ones
five pigtails
two pairs of sneakers
two berets
two smiles
one necklace
one bracelet
lots of stripes and
one good friendship

Associations

EVE MERRIAM

Home to me is not a house
Filled with family faces;
Home is where I slide in free
By rounding all the bases.

A tie to me is not
Clothing like a hat;
It means the game is even up
And I wish I were at bat.

Roberto Clemente

JUDITH BARNARD

Have you ever thought about being two people? When you're in school or talking to friends, that's the *public* you that people see. But you also do things that not everyone knows about. You help a friend in trouble. You do your mother a favor. That's the *private* you that you don't talk about to everyone.

Roberto Clemente was two people. In public he was one of the greatest baseball players who ever lived. He played for the Pittsburgh Pirates for almost twenty years— from 1955 to 1972. He was the eleventh player in major-league history to get 3,000 hits. His lifetime batting average was .317. He was so good that he won four National League batting championships.

Roberto was not just a good hitter. He was also one of the best right fielders in baseball. He won his league's Most Valuable Player award once and the Golden Glove award for fielding twelve times. He was named Outstanding Player in the 1971 World Series. In 1973 he was elected to the National Baseball Hall of Fame.

This was the public Roberto Clemente, the one baseball fans still love and admire.

Who was the private Roberto Clemente? He was a young ball player from Puerto Rico, a stranger in the United States. He knew what it meant to be lonely and afraid. This made him want to help others who were lonely and afraid, especially young people.

Roberto visited sick boys and girls in hospitals all over the country. He set up baseball clinics in Puerto Rico so young people would have something healthy and fun to do after school. He dreamed of and began building a "Sports Center" in his hometown of San Juan. This would be a place where *all* children, rich or poor, could come to learn to play any kind of sport they wanted.

181

Roberto didn't help only young people. In December 1972 he read about an earthquake in Nicaragua, a country in Central America. Thousands of people had been killed in this earthquake. The capital city, Managua, was nothing more than a pile of broken rocks.

"Those people need help," Roberto said. He went to Puerto Rico to collect food, clothing, and medicine to send to Managua. When all of the supplies had been collected, Roberto helped load them onto an old DC-7 airplane at the San Juan airport. The plane was overloaded, but Roberto decided to fly along with the supplies to Nicaragua. He wanted to make sure the people in Managua got the things they needed right away.

So it was the private Roberto Clemente who died on 31 December 1972, when the old plane crashed into the sea. For days, airplanes and helicopters searched for the plane. Deep-sea divers found the plane wreckage in the ocean, but Roberto Clemente was never seen again.

Many people remember the public Roberto Clemente, the outstanding baseball player. They also remember the private Roberto, who always had time to help someone less fortunate than himself. That was the way he lived, and that was the way he died.

Today Is Very Boring

JACK PRELUTSKY

Today is very boring,
it's a very boring day,
there is nothing much to look at,
there is nothing much to say,
there's a peacock on my sneakers,
there's a penguin on my head,
there's a dormouse on my doorstep,
I am going back to bed.

183

Today is very boring,
it is boring through and through,
there is absolutely nothing
that I think I want to do,
I see giants riding rhinos,
and an ogre with a sword,
there's a dragon blowing smoke rings,
I am positively bored.

Today is very boring,
I can hardly help but yawn,
there's a flying saucer landing
in the middle of my lawn,
a volcano just erupted
less than half a mile away,
and I think I felt an earthquake,
it's a very boring day.

184

He Reached for the Stars

ABIGAIL KELLEY

"Robert! Robert! What are you doing?"

Young Robert Goddard was standing on top of a high fence. He had an old, used-up battery in his hand and was getting ready to jump. The five-year-old boy knew that batteries made things go, and he wanted to go up into the sky. Luckily, his mother saw him in time to keep him from having a bad fall.

This was one of the first of Robert's many science experiments. From the time he was a young boy he was interested in how things worked. He built things and studied animals and read many books. Mostly, he was interested in flight and space. When Robert was growing up, the airplane had not yet been invented. Balloons were the only way people could be lifted off the ground. The only rockets people knew about were fireworks and the rockets used to send signals from the decks of ships. None of these flew very high or very far.

Robert watched birds to see whether he could understand what made them fly. He made arrows that

would soar higher than most. He built and flew dozens of
kites. Many of his experiments didn't work, but Robert
never gave up.

One October day when Robert was sixteen years old,
he climbed a cherry tree to trim off its dead branches. As he
looked around at the sky and down at the earth, he began
to daydream. He imagined what it would be like in a
spaceship. The deep blue sky seemed like a great ocean to be
explored. He knew then that it could be done—something
could be made that would put people into space. And he
wanted to get started as soon as possible.

Robert Goddard climbed down from the cherry tree
sure of his goal in life. From that moment, he set out to
reach that goal. First he studied hard and became a scientist.
Then he started building rockets. All the time he kept on
doing experiment after experiment.

Many people thought Goddard was strange. He spent a
lot of time building rockets that blew up or never left the

ground. He wrote an article about his work in which he talked about how people could someday fly to the moon. This made people think he was even stranger. But Robert was not discouraged. He just decided to continue his work without telling people about it.

On 16 March 1926, Robert Goddard was ready for another experiment. In a field on a farm in Massachusetts, he and his wife and two helpers set up his latest, liquid-fueled rocket on its launching stand. Mrs. Goddard was ready with a camera. One helper held a blowtorch to the rocket engine. Dr. Goddard pulled a cord. Everyone waited to see what would happen.

The rocket roared and flamed for a few seconds. Then, slowly, it began to rise. It picked up speed and raced skyward. It flew to a height of 41 feet, reached the speed of 60 miles an hour, and traveled 184 feet. The world's first liquid-fueled rocket had made a successful flight. Thanks to Robert Goddard's hard work, a first small step into space was made on that March day in 1926.

Emma's Dragon Hunt

CATHERINE STOCK

Emma was excited. Her Grandfather Wong from China was coming to live with her family.

But when her grandfather arrived, he didn't look happy.

"The house is right on top of the hill, and the roof is too flat," he grumbled. "I can't live here."

Emma looked at her grandfather, puzzled. "Why not, Grandfather?" she asked.

Grandfather Wong turned around and looked at her. "Because there are sure to be dragons living in the hill under the house. They will dance on the flat roof and keep me awake all night," he said.

That night Emma couldn't sleep.

Mother was cross with Grandfather Wong the next morning. "How can Emma concentrate on her lessons when she hasn't slept because of this dragon nonsense?"

"It's not nonsense," Grandfather Wong answered quietly.

That night when Grandfather Wong came in to say good night, Emma had all her stuffed animals with her in bed.

"You musn't be afraid of the dragons," he said. "Our Chinese dragons are good dragons."

"But what do they look like?" Emma asked nervously.

Grandfather took a deep breath. "A Chinese dragon has the head of a camel, the neck of a snake, the horns of a stag, the eyes of a cat, the ears of a bull, the belly of a clam, the pads of a tiger, the tail of a lizard, the wings and claws of an eagle, the scales of a carp, and the whiskers of Wang Fu, the philosopher."

"Sounds scary to me," whispered Emma.

"No, no. Not at all," Grandfather assured her. "Tomorrow we'll hunt for one. You'll see."

The next morning Emma was so excited that she could hardly wait for Grandfather Wong to finish his second cup of tea.

"Well, now," he said at last. "Dragons like wet and marshy places."

So Emma took Grandfather to see the stream next to the house. She didn't find a dragon, but she did find a ball.

"Dragons love to play ball," said Grandfather Wong. "There must be one close by."

They walked up into the hills. No dragons!

"When it's hot like this, they go underground where it's cooler. These mountains hold many dragon tunnels," explained Grandfather.

Suddenly the earth began to tremble and quake. Emma and her grandfather tumbled down in a heap.

"Was that a dragon?" asked Emma.

Grandfather Wong nodded. "We'll come back tomorrow."

The next day was unusually hot. Emma and Grandfather Wong set off again, hand in hand.

"I made this little paper dragon to put in the sun," he said. "If it gets hot enough, a real dragon sleeping under the hill will wake up."

Everything began to grow dark. Grandfather and
Emma looked up at the sky. The sun was slowly
disappearing!

"Oh, dear," muttered Grandfather. "The dragon is so
angry with the sun for waking him that he is trying to
swallow it. But don't worry. The sun is so hot that he'll
soon spit it out."

And he did. The sun came out again, but billowy clouds of steam had gathered in the sky. They began to darken. Emma and her grandfather ran for cover as thunder boomed across the sky.

"The dragon is still angry," Grandfather shouted above the noise. "He and his friends are knocking the clouds together. Boom! Boom! Luckily, their sharp claws rip open the clouds and let out all the rain."

It rained and it rained and it rained. On Monday morning when Emma was getting ready for school, it was still raining.

"I'll ask Shom the Broom's daughter to sweep away those stormy dragons," Grandfather whispered to Emma. "She's a beautiful, distant star."

"Where will she sweep them?" asked Emma.

"She sweeps them into the sea with all the clouds," Grandfather told her.

"Oh." Emma looked at a button on her raincoat.

"Dragons hunt for pearls in the sea. Their eyes are so sharp that fishermen paint dragon eyes on their boats to help them find fish," said Grandfather.

"I hope the dragons come back," Emma said softly.

When Emma got home from school, a brisk wind had swept all the clouds away. Her grandfather had a surprise for her—a beautiful dragon kite.

"It's to let the dragons know that we are their friends," he said.

At dinner everyone was talking about the things that had happened since Grandfather had arrived. There had been an earthquake, a heat wave, a solar eclipse, and a terrible thunderstorm followed by a beautiful rainbow.

Grandfather and Emma smiled, but they didn't say anything.

Grandfather Wong let Emma hang the kite in her room that night. She lay in bed and, just as she was falling asleep, she was sure that she could hear the pattering of dancing dragons on the roof.

Glossary

Pronunciation Key

a_, ă_	apple, tan	g	gas, wiggle, sag
ā	acorn, table	ġ	gem, giant, gym
à	alone, Donna	gh_	ghost
â	air, care	_gh	though, thought (silent)
ä	father, wand	h_	hat
a̧	all, ball	i_, ĭ_	it, sit
a_e	ape, bake	ī	pilot, pie
ai_	aim, sail	_ï_	babies, machine, *also*
àr	calendar		onion, savior, familiar
är	art, park, car	i_e	ice, bite
au_	author, Paul	_igh	high, bright
aw	awful, lawn, saw	ir	irk, bird, fir
_ay	say, day	j_	jam
b	bat, able, tub	k	kite, ankle, ink
c	cat, cot, cut	kn_	knife
ce	cent, ace	l	lamp, wallet, tail
ch	chest, church	_le	table, ample
c̄h	chorus, ache	m	man, bump, ham
c̆h	chute	_mb	lamb, comb
ci	cider, decide	n	no, tent, sun
_ci_	special	_n̄_	uncle, anger
_ck	tack, sick	_ng	sing, ring
cy	bicycle	o_, ŏ_	odd, pot
d	dad	ō	go, no, toe
_dge	edge, judge	ȯ	come, wagon
e_, ě_	elf, hen	ô	off, song
ē	equal, me	oa_	oat, soap
ė	moment, loaded	o_e	ode, bone
ea	eat, leap, tea	oi_	oil, boil
_ĕa_	head, bread	o͞o	book, nook
ee	eel, feet, see	o͞o	boot, zoo
er	herd, her	or	order, normal
_ew	few, blew	ȯr	motor, doctor
f	far, taffy, off	ou_	out, hound

ow	owl, town, cow	ṳ̄	truth, true
_ōw	low, throw	u̇	nature
_oy	boy, toy	u̲	pull, full
p	paper, tap	ur	urge, turn, fur
ph	phone, elephant, graph	ūr	cure, pure
qu_	quick, queen	v	voice, save
r	ram, born, ear	w_	will, wash
s	sun, ask, yes	wh_	white, what
_s̲	toes, hose	wr_	write
_s̲_	vision, confusion	_x	extra, ax
ss̲	fission	_x_	exist, example
sh	show, bishop, fish	y_	yes, yet
t	tall, sets, bit	_y	baby, happy (when
th	thick, three		it is the only
<u>th</u>	this, feather, bathe		vowel in a final
_tch	itch, patch		unstressed
_<u>ti</u>_	nation, station,		syllable)
	also question	_y̆_	cymbal
ṭu	congratulate	_ȳ	cry, sky
u_, ŭ_	up, bus	y̌	zephyr, martyr
ū	use, cute, *also* granulate	z	zoo, nozzle, buzz

1. If a word ends in a silent *e,* as in **face,** the silent *e* is not marked. If a word ends in -*ed* pronounced **t,** as in **baked,** or **d,** as in **stayed,** no mark is needed. If the ending -*ed* forms a separate syllable pronounced **ėd,** as in **load'ėd,** the *e* has a dot.

2. If there are two or three vowels in the same syllable and only one is marked, as in **beaū'ty, friĕnd, rōgue,** or **breāk,** all the other vowels in the syllable are silent.

3. The Open Court diacritical marks in the Pronunciation Key make it possible to indicate the pronunciation of most unfamiliar words without respelling.

à·blaze' *adj.* on fire

ā'ble *adj.* having the skill to do well

à·cad'è·my *n.* a school at which students learn one main thing

ac'cent *n.* the way words sound when spoken by people from a certain country or area

àc·cus'tòm *v.* to become used to

ad·mire' *v.* to look up to

à·drill'in' *v.* the way some people say "drilling"

à·float' *adj.* on top of water or other liquid

aġe *n.* 1. a great many years 2. how old someone or something is

aim *v.* to plan

À·las'kà *n.* the most northern state in the United States

À·mer'i·càn Rev'ò·lū'tiòn *n.* the war that produced the United States (*See also* **Revolutionary War.**)

Ä'nà·sä'zï *n.* an American Indian tribe in the southwestern United States

An'der·sòn·ville Pri'sòn *n.* a jail for captured northern soldiers during the Civil War

À·pol'lō *n.* a space program named after the ancient god of light

ap'pli·cā'tiòn *n.* a paper having blank spaces on it to be filled in for some special purpose

à·rock'ing *v.* the way some people say "rocking"

àr·rānġe' *v.* to put in place

Ā'sià *n.* one of the seven large bodies of dry land on Earth

às·sō'çi·ā'tiòn *n.* something that comes to mind when a person thinks of another thing

as'trò·naut *n.* a traveler on a spaceship

At·lan'tic O·cean (ō'shàn) *n.* the huge body of water east of North America and South America

ax han'dle *n.* about two feet long (special meaning in this story)

band *n.* a group of people gathered for some purpose

bärk *n.* the outer covering of a tree trunk

bat'ter·y *n.* an object that provides electricity

bay *n.* a place where the sea is partly surrounded by land

beâr *v.* to push or to press

beat'èn *adj.* pounded

Ben'jà·min Frañk'lin *n.* one of the writers of the laws of the United States

be·ret (bė·rā′) *n.* a flat, round hat

Big Dip′per *n.* a group of stars that forms the shape of a long-handled cup

Big Woŏds *n.* a name given to a forest

Bill′ing·ham *n.* a town in Massachusetts

bil′lōw·y *adj.* moving the way large waves do

bit′ter *adj.* difficult to stand; unpleasant

blōw′torch *n.* a tool that has a very hot flame

blue′bon′net *n.* a small wild flower that has blue blossoms

bōul′der *n.* a huge rock

boy′cott *v.* to join with others in refusing to use something

breast′plate *n.* a chest covering worn in battle

Brer *n.* the way some people say "brother"

breech′clôth *n.* a piece of clothing worn around the hips by American Indian men

buck′ėt bri·gade′ *n.* a line of people passing pails of water from hand to hand to fight a fire

buck′skin *n.* soft, deerskin leather

Bue′nôs dí·as (dĭ′äs), **ä·mĭ′gôs** the Spanish words for "good morning, friends"

Pronunciation Key

VOWELS: sat, hăve, āble, fäther, all, câre, àlone; yet, brĕad, mē, loadėd; it, practĭce, pīlot, machĭne; hot, nō, ôff, wagòn; foŏt, foōd; oil, toy; count, town; up, ūse, trŭth, pŭll; mȳth, baby, crȳ, zephýr.

CONSONANTS: cent, cider, cycle; chorus, chute; ġem; light, and though (silent), ghost; iñk; elephant; toes; them; special, measure, nation, nature.

---

buf′fà·lō *n.* a large animal that looks almost like a woolly bull

buñk′house *n.* a building for many people to sleep in

burnt ôf′fer·ing *n.* an object that is set on fire to follow the rules of a religion

Cal′i·for′nï·à *n.* a state on the southwestern coast of the United States

Can′à·dà *n.* the country north of the United States

can′nòn *n.* a kind of large gun

ca·noe (cà·nū′) *n.* a light, narrow boat moved by paddling

cap′i·tàl *adj.* having the main government offices

Cap′i·tòl *n.* the building in Washington, D.C., in which leaders make laws for Americans

Cap′tàin Jones *n.* the captain of the *Mayflower*

cärp *n.* a large fish

cast iron (ī′ern) *adj.* made of iron mixed with hardening materials

cat′·e·̄chis′·ĕm *n.* the teachings of a religion

cease *v.* to stop or to end

ce̅′·dȧr *n.* a kind of evergreen tree with reddish wood and a strong, pleasant smell

cel′·e·̇bra̅′·ti̠ȯn *n.* a party or other special event held in honor of a happy occasion

cham′·pï·ȯn·ship′ *n.* the winning place in a game or contest

c̄hâr′·ac·ter *n.* a person's real self; what makes a person good or bad

Char·bon·neau (shär′bô·no̅) *n.* the French-Canadian who married Sacajawea

chȧrġe *n.* an amount of explosive to be set off all at one time

Chï′nȧ *n.* a huge country close to India and Japan

chore *n.* a small job that must be done over and over

chow′hạll *n.* a building in which many people eat together

C̄hris′·tȯ·pher Cȯ·lum′bus *n.* one of the first people to sail from Europe to North America

cin′der *n.* a small piece of wood or other material that has been burned not quite to ashes

ci′vil rights *n. pl.* the freedom to do what others in a country are allowed to do

Ci′vil Wạr *n.* the war between the northern and the southern parts of the United States

clin′ic *n.* a class that teaches certain skills

coast *n.* the land by the sea or ocean

coast′ȧl *adj.* living in the area where land and sea meet

cob′bler *n.* a person who makes and repairs shoes

cȯl·lec′ti̠ȯn *n.* a group of things that are alike

col′ȯ·nist *n.* a person who settles in a new land

col′ȯ·ny *n.* one of the early settlements in the United States

cȯm·mū′ni·cate *v.* to give and get information

cȯm·pâre′ *v.* to look for likenesses and differences

cȯn·di′ti̠ȯns *n. pl.* facts or events that affect a place

cȯn·duc′tȯr *n.* someone who takes care of passengers on a train

con′fi·dent·ly *adv.* boldly or bravely

con′tent *n.* what is in something

con′ti·nȧ̇t *n.* one of the seven main areas of dry land on Earth

cȯn·tro̅l′ *v.* to hold back or force someone to follow rules

coun'cil *n.* a group of people who make the rules of a community

cour'age *n.* bravery

cra'dle·board' *n.* a plank used to carry a baby on

cra'ter *n.* a cup-shaped hole in the ground

cre·ate' *v.* to make

crea'ture *n.* an animal or person

crew *n.* a group of people who work on a ship or an airplane

dan'ger·ous *adj.* able to cause harm

Dan'iel Boone *n.* a man who led people to live in new areas in North America long ago

Deb'o·rah Samp'son *n.* a young woman who dressed as a man to fight in the American Revolution

dec'la·ra'tion *n.* a statement

de·clare' *v.* to announce

des'ert *n.* a large area of very dry land

de'sire' *n.* a strong wish or a longing

dip'per *n.* a small pan having a long handle

dis'tance *n.* a faraway place

dis'tant *adj.* 1. a long way away 2. far in the past

Do·ña (dô'nyä) **Fe·li'sä** *n.* a woman who was mayor of San Juan, Puerto Rico, for many years

dôr'mouse *n.* a small, furry animal that looks like a squirrel

drill *n.* a special tool used to make holes

drill'in' *v.* the way some people say "drilling"

drought *n.* a long time without enough rain

dug'out' *adj.* made from a hollowed-out tree trunk —*n.* a shelter made by digging a hole in the ground and covering it with a roof

dusk *n.* the time of day just before dark

dȳ'na·mite *n.* a kind of explosive

ed'ū·cāt·èd *adj.* having been taught at school

eld'èst *n.* the oldest in a family

elk *n.* a very large kind of deer

Eng′lånd *n.* a country in Britain, in northern Europe

ē′quål *adj.* allowed by law to do the same things as other people

Eu·rope (yoŏr′ŏp) *n.* a very large body of land west of Asia

ė·rupt′ *v.* to explode

ė·vent′ *n.* a happening

ėx·am′ĭne *v.* to look at carefully

ex·hib·it (ex·ib′it) *n.* a showing or display

ėx·pĕr′i·ment *n.* a test for finding out or trying new ideas

ėx·plore′ *v.* to travel to an unknown place to find out about it

fạl′cȯn *n.* a fast, powerful bird

fam′ĭne *n.* a long period of time during which many people do not have enough food

fā′tȧl *adj.* causing death

feast *n.* a grand meal for many people

Fe·li′sä Rin·cón (riñ·côn′) **de Gau·tier** (gow·tyĕr′) *n.* a woman who was mayor of San Juan, Puerto Rico, for many years

fi′ber *n.* a long, thin piece of a plant

fidġ′ėt *v.* to wiggle around while waiting

fiērce *adj.* strong enough to cause harm

fiñ′ger spell′ing *n.* movements of the hands that mean letters

fire′stick *n.* a long stick used to carry flame from a burning fire to an unlit fire

fire′wȯrks *n. pl.* a show of bright, loud explosives

flap′jack *n.* a pancake

flat′boat *n.* a ship having a wide bottom

Flôr′i·dȧ *n.* the state at the southeastern corner of the United States

flūe *n.* the pipe that carries smoke in a chimney

fog′horn′ *n.* an object that makes a loud sound as a warning to ships in foggy or rainy weather

France *n.* a country in western Europe

freight (frāt) *n.* things carried by trucks, trains, ships, or airplanes between places

fū′tȗre *n.* the time yet to come

gal′lȯp·ing *adj.* running fast

game *n.* wild animals caught for food

ga·rage (gȧ·räs′) *n.* a building or part of a building used for storing cars or trucks

gaze *v.* to look or to stare

ġen′ėr·ȯus *adj.* 1. willing to give or to share 2. large or full

ġen′ė·sis *n.* a beginning

glide *v.* to move in a smooth, easy way

glōw *v.* to give off a soft light

gnarled (närld) *adj.* twisted or covered with bumps

goal *n.* what a person aims for

go͞ods *n. pl.* things bought and sold

gȯv′ern *v.* to make rules for living together

grave′ly *adv.* without joking

grav′i·ty *n.* the power that makes objects fall downward

grāz′ing *adj.* feeding on small, growing plants

Greāt Plains *n.* a large, flat area in the middle of the United States

Greāt Spĭr′its *n. pl.* the gods worshipped by the American Indians

grub *n.* an insect that is not fully grown (A grub looks like a short, thick worm.)

guīde *n.* a leader into new places —*v.* to lead others into new places

Gulf Stream *n.* an area of warm water in the cold, northern part of the Atlantic Ocean

---

Pronunciation Key

VOWELS: sat, hăve, āble, fäther, all, câre, ȧlone; yet, brĕad, mē, loadėd; it, practĭce, pīlot, machīne; hot, nō, ȯff, wagȯn; fo͝ot, fo͞od; oil, toy; count, town; up, ūse, trŭth, pu̶ll; mȳth, baby, crȳ, zephȳr.

CONSONANTS: cent, cider, cycle; c̄horus, c̆hute; ġem; light, and though (silent), ghost; iñk; elephant; toes̱; t̲hem; special, measu̱re, nation, natu̱re.

---

här′bȯr *n.* a protected place along a shore

härd′ship *n.* something that is painful or difficult

här·po͞on′ *n.* a large spear with a sharp point

här′vėst *n.* the food gathered from crops

hatch′ėt *n.* a tool with a short handle and a sharp blade for chopping or cutting

heal′ing *adj.* making well

heave *v.* to pull up with great difficulty

hĕr′ring *n.* a shiny, blue-green and black fish

Hĭ·dät′sä *n.* an American Indian tribe living along the Missouri River

high hopes *n. pl.* grand visions

hill′ȯck *n.* a small mound of earth

hinġed *adj.* having a metal part that allows for bending back

his′tȯ·ry *n.* all that has happened in the past

hitch′ing *v.* strapping an animal to an object to be pulled

hol′i·day *n.* a day set aside to honor some special event or person

Hol′lànd *n.* a country in western Europe

hol′ler *v.* to yell

home′stĕad′ *v.* to come to own land by settling on it

im·mē′dĭ·àte·ly *adv.* at once

im′mi·grànt *n.* a person who comes to live in a country

im·prove (im·prū̄v′) *v.* to make better

in′dė·pend′ènce *n.* freedom

In′dĭ·à *n.* a country in the southeastern part of Asia

In′dĭ·àn *n.* a member of the first race of people who lived in North and South America

In′dieṣ *n.* an old name for the area of Japan, China, and India

in·dus′trĭ·àl *adj.* having many factories

iñk well *n.* a small jar filled with ink for old-fashioned pens

in′stru·mènt *n.* a tool used for doing a certain kind of work

in·vent′ *v.* to make or think of something new

in·ven′tiòn *n.* a new tool, machine, or way of doing something

Ī′ȯ·wȧ *n.* a state in the middle part of the United States

Ī′rish *adj.* from the country of Ireland

It′à·ly *n.* a country in the southern part of Europe

Jȧ·pan′ *n.* a country in Asia near China and India

joùr′nȧl *n.* a diary

joùr′nēy *n.* a long trip, mostly on land

Ju·ni·pe·ro (hū′nĭ·pe′rô) **Ser′rä** *n.* a priest who came to California from Mexico to build churches and schools

ker′nėl *n.* a seed; a grain

kill *n.* the animals brought back from hunting

knuck′le *n.* the place where a finger bends

land bridge *n.* a narrow strip of land that joins two large ones

Land hō! words called out by the first sailor who sees land during a long trip on the ocean

launch *v.* to start or send off

launch′ing stand *n.* a platform that holds up a rocket before it is sent into space

lay *v.* to arrange materials for

leġ'ėnd *n.* a story told and retold for many years

lib'er·ty *n.* freedom to think and act as a person wishes

lō'cȯ·mō'tĭve *n.* the engine of a train

Lo·de·wyk (lō·dė·vek') **Pôs**

lodge *n.* an American Indian shelter

lông'house *n.* a shelter built by American Indians for several families to live in together

lông'ing·ly *adv.* with a wish to be a part of something

Loū·ĭ·sï·an'ȧ *n.* a state in the southeastern United States

Lṵ̄·ĭs' Mu·ñoz (mṵ̄·nyōs') **Ma·rín** (mä·rïn') *n.* the first elected governor of Puerto Rico

Ly̆s̲'bet

Ma·ha'la

maize *n.* corn

man'aġe *v.* to be able

Ma·na·gua (mä·nä'gwä) *n.* the capital city of Nicaragua

mȧ·nūre' *n.* the solid waste from animals

Mȧ·rï'ȧ Mar·ti·nez (mär·tï'nes̲) *n.* an American Indian artist

märks'mȧn·ship' *n.* skill with a gun or bow

märsh'y *adj.* having patches of wet ground

mär'vėl·ȯus *adj.* wonderful

Mâr'y Cȧs·satt' *n.* an American artist famous for her paintings of women and children

Mas'sȧ·chṳ'setts *n.* a state in the northeastern United States

mȧ·tē'rï·ȧl *n.* what an object is made from

Mȧ'ti'ni·cus

May'flow·er *n.* the name of the first ship that brought people from Europe to North America

meal *n.* a form of corn that is dried and ground up

mend'ing *n.* clothing that needs to be repaired

meth'ȯd *n.* a way of doing something

Mex'·i·cō *n.* the country south of the United States

mī'cȧ *n.* a soft rock that splits easily into thin, sparkling sheets

midst *n.* the middle of a group

Min′nė·sō′tà *n.* a state in the northern United States

mi·rac′ū·lòus *adj.* impossible to explain; amazing

mis′sion *n.* a group of buildings used by people bringing religion to a new land

Mis′sis·sip′pï Riv′er *n.* the longest river in the United States

moc′cà·sin *n.* an American Indian shoe having a soft sole

mōōn′quake *n.* a shaking and cracking of the surface of the moon

Mō′ses *n.* a great leader told about in the Bible

mō′tion·lèss *adj.* without moving

mound *n.* a low hill

Mound Buil·ders (bild′ers) *n. pl.* American Indian tribes that lived in parts of the eastern United States

mush *n.* a soft food somewhat like oatmeal

mūte *adj.* unable to speak

mўs′ter·y *n.* a secret

nag *v.* to repeat many times

Na′tion·àl League (leag) *n.* a certain group of baseball teams

nā′tĭve *adj.* having to do with where a person is born

nat′ū·ràl *adj.* coming from the outdoor world

nā′tùre *n.* part of what an animal or person is really like

Nė·bras′kà *n.* a state in the middle of the United States

neigh·bor·hood (nā′bòr·hōod) *n.* the area near a house or other place

net′ting *n.* a cloth having open spaces between the threads

net′tle *n.* a plant that is covered with fine hairs

New Am′ster·dam *n.* an old name for New York

New Or′lē·àns (*or* or·lēns′) *n.* a city in Louisiana

Nī·ag′à·rà Falls *n.* the widest waterfall in the world (Niagara Falls touches both the United States and Canada)

Ni·ca·ra·gua (ni·cà·rä′gwä) *n.* a country in Central America

Nic·ò·dē′mus *n.* a town in Kansas

night′in·gale *n.* a bird that sings its pleasant song mainly after dark

Ni·ña (nïn′yä) *n.* one of the three ships that carried Columbus and his crew to North America

North À·mer′i·cà *n.* one of the seven large bodies of land on Earth

ob′ject *n.* a thing that can be seen —**ob·ject′** *v.* to argue against

odds and ends *n. pl.* bits and pieces

o·gre (ō′ger) *n.* a make-believe monster

O·hī′ō Riv′er *n.* a river that flows to the Mississippi River

O′mȧ·hä′ *n.* a city in Nebraska

ō′pėn *v.* to make ready —*adj.* not fenced off

or′chȧrd *n.* a group of trees grown for fruit

O·saġe′ (*or* ō′saġe) *n.* an American Indian tribe living in the middle of the United States

out′cȯme *n.* the last thing that happens

Pȧ·cif′ic O·cean (ō′shȧn) *n.* the huge body of water west of North America and South America

pad *n.* the soft bottom of an animal's foot

paġ′ėant *n.* a grand performance or show

pal′ȧce *n.* a place fancy enough for a king or a queen

pȧ·rade′ *n.* a line of people marching through the streets in time to music

Pâ′ris *n.* the capital city of France

pass *n.* a way across mountains

patch *n.* a small area; a spot

pā′trï·ȯt *n.* a person who loves his or her country

pat′tern *n.* a repeated design

peak *n.* the pointed top of a mountain

pėarl *n.* a smooth, round, white jewel that comes from an oyster

peg fŏŏt *n.* a wooden foot

per′mȧ·nėnt *adj.* meant to last

pet′tï·coat *n.* a thin skirt worn under another skirt or dress

Phil′ȧ·del′phï·ȧ *n.* a large city in Pennsylvania

phi·los′ȯ·pher *n.* a person who studies ideas about life

Pil′grim *n.* a person who came from Europe long ago to live in North America

Pïn′tä *n.* one of the three ships that carried Columbus and his crew to North America

pī·ȯ·neer′ *n.* one of the first people to live in a new land

plain *n.* a large area of flat land

plank *n.* a movable board that people use as a bridge between ship and land

plaque (plak) *n.* a metal or stone sign

plen'ti·ful *adj.* more than enough in number

Plym'outh *n.* a city in Massachusetts

poi'son *n.* a thing that can cause sickness or death

pos·ses'sion *n.* something owned

pos'sum *n.* a small long-nosed animal that lives in trees (*Also spelled* o·pos'sum.)

pot'ter·y *n.* objects made from dried earth

Po·ve·ka (pō·vā'kà) *n.* the real name of Maria Martinez

prâi'rie *n.* a large, flat grassland

pride *n.* what makes a person think well of himself of herself

Prom'on·tō'ry *n.* a town in Utah

prō'test *v.* to give reasons against

Pueb·lo (pweb'lō) *n.* an American Indian tribe living in the southwestern United States

purr *v.* to make a low, murmuring sound showing pleasure

pur·suit' *n.* what is done to try to get or to find something

puz'zled-like' *adj.* confused

quail *n.* a small, plump bird hunted for food

Queen Is·à·bel'là *n.* the Spanish ruler who gave Columbus ships

quake *v.* to shake

quiv'er *n.* a case for holding arrows

rail'road *n.* the tracks that trains run on

rails *n. pl.* the metal pieces that trains run on

ram'ble *v.* to wander around

rän'chō *n.* the Spanish word for "ranch"

rap'id *n.* a fast part of a river

rat'tle watch *n.* a group of fire fighters (A rattle was shaken to call the fire fighters.)

raw'hide *adj.* made from cowskin

red'wood *n.* a kind of tree that grows only on the West Coast of the United States

reed *n.* the dried stem of a tall water plant

rè·form' *n.* improvement

rè·fūse' *v.* to say no to

reg'i·ment *n.* a group of soldiers that is part of an army

reg'is·ter *v.* to sign a list

rè·li'gion *n.* a way of worshiping

rè·store' *v.* to bring back

re·tire' *v.* to give up working, usually after a certain age

rev'o·lu'tion *n.* the end of an old government and start of a new, often with war (*See also* **American Revolution** *and* **Revolutionary War.**)

Rev'o·lu'tion·ar·y War *n.* the war in which the United States broke ties with England (*See also* **American Revolution.**)

rich *adj.* 1. having more than is needed 2. able to produce good crops

roam *v.* to travel a long way

Rob'ert God'dard *n.* a person who is famous for work with rockets

Rob'ert Shurt'leff *n.* a false name used by Deborah Sampson

Ro·ber'to Cle·men'te *n.* a famous baseball player

roll'ing *adj.* rising and falling, as small hills

Ru'fus Mof'fat

run'ner *n.* a sharp, metal strip that makes sliding an object on snow easy

Sab'bath *n.* the day of rest and worship

Sac'a·ja·we'a *n.* a woman of the Shoshoni tribe who helped Lewis and Clark reach the Pacific Ocean

Sac'ra·men'to *n.* the capital city of California

sac'ri·fice *v.* to give gifts to the gods, often of living or once-living things

sail'or *n.* a person who travels on the ocean for a living

salm·on (sam'on) *n.* a kind of pink or red fish caught for food

Sän Juan (hwän) *n.* the capital city of Puerto Rico

Sän'tä Mä·ri'ä *n.* one of the three ships that carried Columbus and his crew to North America

sap *n.* the juice that flows in plants and trees

saw'mill *n.* a place where logs are sawed into boards

scale *n.* one of the thin pieces of skin that cover a fish

scarce'ly *adv.* only with difficulty

scī'en·tist *n.* a person who looks for answers to questions about the world

scout *n.* a person who is sent ahead to find out something

209

sea ot'ter *n.* a furry ocean animal

sea ser'pent *n.* a make-believe ocean monster

sense *n.* the ability to see, hear, smell, taste, or touch —*v.* to come to know

sē'ri·ous·ly *adv.* in a way that shows the importance of something

ser'mon *n.* a speech in church given by a minister

serv'ant *n.* a person who does work in another's home

set'tle *v.* to make a home

set'tler *n.* a person who comes to live in a new land

shā'man *n.* an American Indian who is both doctor and minister

She-Who-Is-A·lone (she–hoo–is–a·lone') *n.* a name that means "a child who is not with parents"

Shīn'ing Moun'tains *n.* the name Sacajawea gave the Rocky Mountains

Shō·shō'nē *or* **Shō·shō'nï** *n.* an American Indian tribe living between Wyoming and California

shrill *adj.* high and sharp in sound

Si·er'ra Ne·vad'a *n.* the name of a line of mountains in eastern California

sight *v.* to see for the first time

sim'ple *adj.* plain

Sioux (soo) *n.* an American Indian tribe living in Minnesota, North Dakota, and South Dakota

skill'ful *adj.* very good at doing something

skimp'y *adj.* not so much as someone might want

slath'er *v.* to spread on thickly

slave *n.* a person who is owned by and works for another person

slāv'er·y *n.* the buying and selling of human beings

slith'er *v.* to slide along in a wiggling way

smōl'der *v.* to burn without bursting into flame

snōw'clad *adj.* covered with snow

snug *adj.* warmly comfortable

sod *n.* the top part of the soil

sōl'ar e·clipse' *n.* a darkening of the sun that lasts a short time

sol'emn (sol'em) *adj.* without cheerfulness

sol'emn·ly (sol'em·ly) *adv.* without joking

soot *n.* a fine, dark powder left by burning material

space prō'gram *n.* a plan for space travel

Spain *n.* a country in southern Europe, near Italy

Span′ish *adj..* having to do with the country, or the language spoken by the people, of Spain—*n. pl.* people from Spain or those who speak the same language

spêar *v.* to stick with a pointed object

spĭr′it *n.* courage to do something dangerous or difficult

spir·it·u·al (spĭr′i·chu̱·ȧl) *n.* a simple, religious song

Squän′to *n.* a member of the Patuxet tribe who helped some of the first Europeans in North America

stag *n.* a full-grown male deer

stam·pēde′ *n.* the sudden running of a group of frightened animals

stā′ti̱o̱n *n.* a stopping place for trains —*v.* to give a soldier or sailor a place for living and working

steep *adj.* almost straight up and down

stream *n.* a small river

stretch *v.* to reach or spread from one place to another

strug′gle *v.* to try in spite of difficulty

stub′bo̱rn *adj.* wanting one's own way

Pronunciation Key

VOWELS: sat, hăve, āble, fäther, ȧll, câre, ȧlone; yet, brĕad, mē, loadèd; it, practĭce, pīlot, machĭne; hot, nō, ôff, wago̱n; fo͞ot, fo͞od; oil, toy; count, town; up, ūse, tru̱th, pu̱ll; mȳth, baby, crȳ, zephȳr.

CONSONANTS: cent, cider, cycle; c̄horus, c̲hute; ġem; light, and though (silent), ghost; iñk; elephant; toe̱s; t̲hem; spec̲ial, mea̱sure, nati̱on, natu̱re.

stump *n.* the part of a tree left above ground after the tree has been cut down

Stuȳ′ver

suc·ceed′ *v.* to do what one has been trying to do, not to fail

sup·plȳ′ *v.* to provide —*n.* an object needed for living or working

sur′fȧce *n.* the outside part

sur·vive′ *v.* to keep on living

swämp′y *adj.* covered with areas of wet ground

swiv′ȅl *n.* a metal part that helps something to turn or rock

tame *v.* to teach an animal to carry a rider

tan *v.* to spank (special meaning)

tap *v.* to make a hole for gathering the liquid that flows in a tree

târ′ri̱·er *n.* an Irish worker who helped build the first railroad across the United States

tax *n.* money paid to run the government

tay *n.* the way some people say "tea"

tel′e·scope *n.* a tool, in the shape of a long tube, that makes faraway things look close

tē′pee *n.* an American Indian tent (*Also spelled* **tipi.**)

Tex′as *n.* a very large state in the southwestern United States

thatch *n.* a covering of straw or leaves

thatched *adj.* covered with a roof made from straw or leaves

Tho′mas (to′mas) **Jef′fer·son** *n.* the third president of the United States

thrive *v.* to grow large and strong

thrust *v.* to push forward, hard

thud *v* to make a loud, dull sound

ti′pi *n.* an American Indian tent (*Also spelled* **tepee.**)

Tō-kï-i-lä-lä-hu̱-wō the Sioux Indian words that mean "Where are you?"

tō′tem pole *n.* a post carved into the shapes of real and imaginary beings, one on top of the other

track *v.* to follow the marks or prints of

trade *v.* to exchange for money or other items

trade′märk *n.* a special object that a person is known for

trap′per *n.* a person who catches animals for their fur

trea′ty *n.* an agreement between groups of people or between countries

tribe *n.* a group of people who live the same way

trim *v.* to cut back or shorten

trol′lēy *n.* a streetcar that runs by electricity

trou′ble *v.* to bother —*n.* a thing that upsets a person

Tus·cum′bï·a *n.* a town in Alabama

′twa̱s *v.* an old-fashioned way to say "it was"

un·con′sci̱ous *adj.* in a kind of sleep

Un′ïon *n.* the group of states called the United States; during the Civil War, the northern states

U·nīt′ed States *n.* the country that lies mainly between Canada and Mexico

urge *v.* to encourage or to try to talk [someone] into

val′ū·a·ble *adj.* important or highly thought of

val′ūed *adj.* loved; worth very much

ven′i·sòn *n.* deer meat

vet′er·àn *n.* a person who has fought in a war

vī′ò·lènce *n.* great force or harmful actions

vī′sòr *n.* the part of a hat that protects the eyes from the sun; a brim that can be seen through

voy′àge *n.* a long trip by sea

Wang Fū

war′rï·òr *n.* fighter (in this case, American Indian)

wat′er·way *n.* a body of water that can be traveled on between places

white′cap *n.* a curling wave with white foam on top

wick *n.* a braided thread, in an oil lamp or a candle, that is burned to make light

wid′ōw *n.* a woman whose husband has died

wig′wäm *n.* a kind of cone-shaped, American Indian house made of poles covered with cloth or skins

Wil′lïàm Brew′ster *n.* a leader of the first Europeans to come to live in North America

wòr′ship *v.* to follow certain beliefs

Pronunciation Key

VOWELS: sat, hăve, āble, fäther, all, câre, àlone; yet, brĕad, mē, loadèd; it, practĭce, pīlot, machĭne; hot, nō, ôff, wagòn; fŏŏt, fōōd; oil, toy; count, town; up, ūse, trŭŭth, pŭll; mȳth, baby, crȳ, zephȳr.

CONSONANTS: cent, cider, cycle; c̄horus, c̱hute; g̣em; light, and though (silent), ghost; iñk; elephant; toeş; ṯhem; special, meaşure, nat̲ion, nat̲ure.

woŭnd *n.* an injury

wreck′àge *n.* what is left of something that has been ruined

yē *pron. pl.* an old-fashioned way to say "you"